a beginner's guide

KRISTYNA ARCARTI

Hodder & Stoughton

A MEMBER OF THE HODDER HEADLINE GROUP

Orders: please contact Bookpoint Ltd, 39 Milton Park, Abingdon, Oxon OX14 4TD.
Telephone: (44) 01235 400414, Fax: (44) 01235 400454. Lines are open from
9.00–6.00, Monday to Saturday, with a 24-hour message answering service.
Email address: orders@bookpoint.co.uk

British Library Cataloguing in Publication Data
A catalogue record for this title is available from The British Library

ISBN 0 340 73753 0

First published 1994
This edition published 1999
Impression number   10 9 8 7 6 5 4 3 2 1
Year   2004 2003 2002 2001 2000 1999

Typeset by Wearset, Boldon, Tyne and Wear
Printed in Great Britain for Hodder & Stoughton Educational, a division of Hodder
Headline Plc, 338 Euston Road, London NW1 3BH by Cox & Wyman Ltd, Reading,
Berkshire

Titles in this series

Astral Projection   Is it possible for the soul to leave the body at will? In this book the traditional techniques used to achieve astral projection are described in a simple, practical way, and Out of the Body and Near Death Experiences are also explored.

Astrology   An exploration of how astrology helps us to understand ourselves and other people. Learn how to draw up and interpret a horoscope.

Astrology and Health   This book explains simply the symbolic richness of the zodiac signs and how they can illuminate our experience of health.

Becoming Prosperous   A guide to how *anyone* can feel and become more prosperous by focusing on state of mind and conscious thought. Practical exercises help readers develop personal strategies to become more prosperous, both financially and emotionally.

Body and Mind Reading   People do not always say what they really feel. Learn to read people's body language and begin to understand what is really going on in their mind. This book is a comprehensive introduction to body language.

Chakras   The body's energy centres, the chakras, can act as gateways to healing and increased self-knowledge. This book shows you how to work with chakras in safety and with confidence.

Channelling   Channelling is the process by which ancient knowledge and wisdom are tapped and reclaimed for the enlightenment and enrichment of life in the present. This book offers simple techniques to become channels of awareness.

Chinese Horoscopes   In the Chinese system of horoscopes, the year of birth is all-important. *Chinese Horoscopes* tells you how to determine your own Chinese horoscope, what personality traits you are likely to have, and how your fortunes may fluctuate in years to come.

Crystal Healing   This book introduces you to the fascinating subject of crystals and gives practical guidance on how to use them safely and how to make them work for you. Discover their healing qualities and how you can use crystals to improve your health.

Dowsing   People all over the world have used dowsing since the earliest times. This book shows how to start dowsing – what to use, what to dowse, and what to expect when subtle energies are detected.

Dream Interpretation   This fascinating introduction to the art and science of dream interpretation explains how to unravel the meaning behind dream images to interpret your own and other people's dreams.

Earth Mysteries   What can we learn from observing the earth and the remains of our prehistoric ancestors? Explore ley lines, earth energies, astro-archaeology and sacred landscapes to expand your consciousness and achieve a better perspective on existence.

Enlightenment   Learn how you can experience primary enlightenment through tried-and-tested exercises which offer the tools to help you to find your own unique truth.

Feng Shui   This beginner's guide to the ancient art of luck management will show you how to increase your good fortune and well-being by harmonising your environment with the natural energies of the earth.

Freeing Your Intuition   Develop awareness of your intuition and make your own good fortune, increase your creative output and learn to recognise what you *know*, not just what you think.

Gems and Crystals   For centuries gems and crystals have been used as an aid to healing and meditation. This guide tells you all you need to know about choosing, keeping and using stones to increase your personal awareness and improve your well-being.

Ghosts   In this exploration of the shadowy world of ghosts, the author looks at poltergeists, hauntings, ghouls, phantoms of the living, the ouija board, ghost hunting, scientific proof of survival after death and the true meaning of Hallowe'en.

The Goddess   This book traces the development, demise and rebirth of the Goddess, looking at the worship of Her and retelling myths from all over the world.

Graphology   Graphology, the science of interpreting handwriting to reveal personality, is now widely accepted and used throughout the world. This introduction will enable you to make a comprehensive analysis of your own and other people's handwriting to reveal the hidden self.

The Healing Powers of Plants   Plants and herbs can be used to enhance everyday life through aromatherapy, herbalism, homoeopathy and colour therapy. Their power can be used in cosmetics, meditation and home decoration.

Herbs for Magic and Ritual   This book looks at the well-known herbs and the stories attached to them. There is information on the use of herbs in essential oils and incense, and on their healing and magical qualities.

I Ching   The roots of *I Ching* or the *Book of Changes* lie in the time of the feudal mandarin lords of China, but its traditional wisdom is still relevant today. Using the original poetry in its translated form, this introduction traces its history, survival and modern-day applications.

Interpreting Signs and Symbols   The history of signs and symbols is traced in this book from their roots to the modern age. It also examines the way psychiatry uses symbolism, and the significance of doodles.

The Language of Flowers   Flowers can and do heal us, both emotionally and physically, with their smell and their beauty. By looking at these areas, together with superstitions associated with flowers and their links with New Age subjects, the author gives advice on how to enhance your life with flowers.

Love Signs   This is a practical introduction to the astrology of romantic relationships. It explains the different roles played by each of the planets, focusing particularly on the position of the Moon at the time of birth.

The Magic and Mystery of Trees   This book explores the many meanings of trees, from myth and folklore through ritual and seasonal uses to their 'spiritual essence' and esoteric meanings.

Meditation   This beginner's guide gives simple, clear instructions to enable you to start meditating and benefiting from this ancient mental discipline immediately. The text is illustrated throughout by full-colour photographs and line drawings.

Mediumship   Whether you want to become a medium yourself, or simply understand what mediumship is about, this book will give you the grounding to undertake a journey of discovery into the spirit realms.

The Moon and You The phase of the Moon when you were born radically affects your personality. This book looks at nine lunar types – how they live, love, work and play, and provides simple tables to find out the phase of your birth.

Money Signs Your money-handling behaviour is influenced by your astrological sign and by the movement of the planets. Learn how to analyse your spending patterns and discover ways to help yourself to improve your financial acumen.

Norse Tradition This book gives a comprehensive introduction to the Norse Tradition, a vibrant living current within the multitude of spiritual paths of paganism.

Numerology Despite being scientifically based, numerology requires no great mathematical talents to understand. This introduction gives you all the information you will need to understand the significance of numbers in your everyday life.

Numerology and Relationships This guide takes you step by step through the hidden meanings behind the important numbers in your life to discover more about you, your compatibilities with others and the crucial relationships with your parents, partner and children.

Pagan Gods for Today's Man Looking at ancient gods and old stories, this guide explores the social and psychological issues affecting the role of men today. In these pages men of all ages and persuasions can find inspiration.

Paganism Pagans are true Nature worshippers who celebrate the cycles of life. This guide describes pagan fesivals and rituals and takes a detailed look at the many forms of paganism practised today.

Palmistry Palmistry is the oldest form of character reading still in use. This illustrated guide shows you exactly what to look for and how to interpret what you find.

Qabalah The Qabalah is an ancient Jewish system of spiritual knowledge centred on the Tree of Life. This guide explains how it can be used in meditation and visualisation, and links it to the chakras, yoga, colour therapy, crystals, Tarot and numerology.

Reiki In this book you will find advice on how to learn Reiki, its application and potential, and you will be shown an avenue of understanding of this simple, practical technique which offers pain relief through meditation and laying-on of hands.

Reincarnation and You What happens to us after death? Here, you will find practical advice on using dreams, recurrent visions, déjà vu and precognition to access hidden parts of your consciousness which recall or anticipate past and future lives.

Runes The power of the runes in healing and giving advice about relationships and life in general has been acknowledged since the time of the Vikings. This book shows how runes can be used in our technological age to increase personal awareness and stimulate individual growth.

Seeing the Future Do you want to change your future, to improve your life now and tomorrow? If so, the ancient arts of prediction can help. This guide is a detailed, practical introduction to divinatory techniques.

Sex Signs A good sex life has been shown to make people happier and healthier. Simply by knowing your birthday and the birthday of a loved one, you can learn about sexuality, needs, seduction tricks and self-expression.

Shamanism Shamanic technique offers direct contact with Spirit, vivid self-knowledge and true kinship with plants, animals and the planet Earth. This book describes the shamanic way, the wisdom of the Medicine Wheel and power animals.

Some Traditional African Beliefs   Fortune telling and healing are two of the aspects of traditional African spiritual life looked at in this book. Exercises based on ancient beliefs show you how to use the environment to find ways to harmonise modern urban life in a practical way.

Spells and Rituals   Rituals are evident in most aspects of life, daily and seasonal rituals, rites of passage, marriage, blessing, popular superstitions. Learn to cast your own spells and make your own rituals, and use them as a means of focusing your mind, altering your consciousness and bringing about creative change.

Spiritual Healing   All healing starts with self, and the Universal Power which makes this possible is available to everyone. In this book there are exercises, techniques and guidelines to follow which will enable you to heal yourself and others spiritually.

Star Signs   This detailed analysis looks at each of the star signs in turn and reveals how your star sign affects everything about you. This book shows you how to use this knowledge in your relationships and in everyday life.

Tantric Sexuality   Tantric Buddhists use sex as a pleasurable path to enlightenment. This guide offers a radically different and exciting new dimension to sex, explaining practical techniques in a clear and simple way.

Tarot   Tarot cards have been used for many centuries. This guide gives advice on which sort to buy, where to get them and how to use them. The emphasis is on using the cards positively, as a tool for gaining self-knowledge, while exploring present and future possibilities.

Visualisation   This introduction to visualisation, a form of self-hypnosis widely used by Buddhists, will show you how to practise the basic techniques – to relieve stress, improve your health and increase your sense of personal well-being.

Witchcraft   This guide to the ancient religion based on Nature worship answers many of the questions and uncovers the myths and misconceptions surrounding witchcraft. Mystical rituals and magic are explained and there is advice for the beginner on how to celebrate the Sabbats.

Working With Colour   Colour is the medicine of the future. This book explores the energy of each colour and its significance, gives advice on how colour can enhance our well-being, and gives ideas on using colour in the home and garden.

Your Psychic Powers   Are you psychic? This book will help you find out by encouraging you to look more deeply within yourself. Psychic phenomena such as precognitive dreams, out of body travels and visits from the dead are also discussed in this ideal stepping stone towards a more aware you.

TO LEN
AS HE WAITS WITHIN VALHÖLL

CONTENTS

INTRODUCTION

Runes originate in the Viking period, in the time of Odin, the chief god of Norse mythology, a time when longboats sailed from the fjords of Scandinavia on military missions. It is part of Viking legend that Odin's horse, Sleipnir, had runic symbols engraved upon its teeth. Maybe for this reason, the 19th rune is called Ehwaz, the horse.

Fortunately runes and runic symbols did not die with the Vikings. Thanks to television and film, many people who would otherwise know nothing of the Vikings are aware of them, their gods and their lifestyle, but relatively few also know that the lore of the Vikings continues well into our modern-day lives through the use of the runes.

Every rune symbolises not only an alphabetical letter, but a deeper meaning, an energy. It is our aim to show the relevance of the wisdom of the runes even in this day and age in our everyday lives as we progress through this book. At the end of the day, wisdom is ageless and its source never dries up.

What is the Futhark?

Runes are often called the Futhark, Futhorc or Elder Futhark after the first six letters of the runic alphabet in traditional order. The runic alphabet has undergone various changes over the years, and runic characters are not only the alphabet of their time but also have their own meanings. They are not mere letters with sounds, and in many ways are similar in character to ancient Egyptian or Hebrew.

Those who are interested in language foundation may already know that runic was originally the language of the northern Germanic races, and that there are remarkable similarities between runic and other early languages, such as early Celtic. Stemming from an unwritten language, the runic symbols were often regarded as magical.

All the characters of the runic alphabet are in straight lines, as with the Ogham alphabet, of which we will learn a little more at a later stage. This is probably because it made them easier to carve on stone.

As we progress with our studies of the runes, we will link the runic symbol with its modern English alphabetical equivalent.

What are runes?

Runes are both strangely marked standing stones found in Scandinavia (more correctly known as runestones rather than runes) and also smaller stones or wooden pieces used as a tool towards self-knowledge and self-help. There are some fine examples of runestones in Stockholm Museum.

Many runic carvings can still be found throughout Europe, but unfortunately some of the original carvings, many made in wood, have now perished, and only the stone carvings remain.

Until relatively recently, runes were seldom heard of and seldom used outside Scandinavia. Readers of Tolkien may have heard of runes, but few people understood their significance. However, their very accessible symbolism began to attract more attention towards the end of the 1960s, and today many people around the world are using them.

Unfortunately the traditional meanings of the runes and their uses have been lost in time, and modern interpretations have had to be formulated. However, as with the Tarot, the runes lend themselves

to the use of intuition, and most modern runemasters rely heavily on this faculty.

The meaning of runes

The word *rune* (sometimes also seen as *run*, *runa* or *runar*) actually means 'secret', 'whisper' or 'mystery', and it is therefore probably no surprise that the original meanings were never written down, just as the Kabbala in Hebrew/Chaldean times was never written down, but passed on by word of mouth.

The fact, however, that the runic symbols were at least carved in rocks meant that they survived, both as a means of communication and as a means of self-enquiry, or as the Vikings thought, a means of getting in touch with the gods.

Thinking in terms of symbolism

Runes have links with many other forms, and are very much in tune with I Ching (the Chinese Book of Changes). It is fair to say that in a sense they were the I Ching of the Viking race. Just as I Ching is concerned with polarities, so are runes, but whereas in I Ching the polarities are termed yin and yang, in runic lore they are fire and ice – images easily understood by the Vikings.

As with Tarot symbolism, which does not end with the picture, runic symbolism does not stop with the outline of the character. The hope is that the drawing or casting of the runes will produce information enabling us to access our own unconscious, thus expanding our awareness and shedding light on our options.

Runes can help with what modern-day psychologists call 'the learning process'. They carry inner meanings which go far beyond their initial appearance and shape. They will give honest answers, but sometimes these answers may not be what we want or expect.

The trick is, at such times, to learn from that answer and to broaden our horizons and experiences. Maybe our destiny lies in a different direction to that which we would wish.

Symbolism can suggest many meanings; the aim in using the runes is to allow the symbolism to permeate the very heart of our being and contact the essence of man.

Runes can help to form a bridge between our logical thinking mind, and that part of ourselves which few understand, but so many wish to find.

Asking questions

Whatever you seek an answer on, you can consult the runes for their wisdom. The question need not have great worldly significance, and may even be fairly trivial – though never frivolous. The main emphasis should be on the need for an answer. Whilst purists would say that one should not ask the runes questions pertaining to the future (such as whether something is likely to turn out well or not), questions can range from 'Should I think of moving house now?' to something more profound that involves spiritual or emotional needs.

The only time you are unlikely to get a straightforward answer is if the blank rune appears, in which case the situation is likely to be in a state of flux, or it is too early to judge the issue effectively. We will look at the blank rune later.

Want to be a runemaster?

It is said that the last great runemasters perished in Iceland in the seventeenth century. The first were most likely priests and priestesses, or wise men or women, who probably cast runestaves (pieces of wood on which runic symbols were drawn).

We have come a long way since then, and runes are now readily available in many commercial outlets, and come in all shapes and

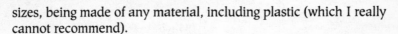

sizes, being made of any material, including plastic (which I really cannot recommend).

Hopefully, by reading this book you will become interested in runes, perhaps sufficiently to want to become a runemaster. Should this not be the case, you will at the very least have helped to establish a link between your conscious and unconscious, which you may choose to develop at a future date.

THE RUNES –
HISTORY AND USE

*R*unes can be used in many ways, but are mainly used nowadays as tools to help us understand a little more about ourselves and also to tap into the energies we all possess within us. Runes teach us to know ourselves, and could be regarded as both teachers and tools. This chapter looks at the history of the runes, and at their use, ancient and modern.

WHAT RUNES CAN DO

Runes are not infallible, are not a supernatural oracle, and are noth 'g to fear. The runic alphabet, whilst said by many both past and present to carry a magical quality, is a means to self-awareness and self-development.

Runes are said by some to carry strong healing vibrations, to protect their owner and to help with finances. It will be up to the reader to decide for themselves on these points. One thing, however, should be made clear from the outset: runes are not a game and should be taken seriously. Don't mess about with runes; they are not toys.

As we have already mentioned, the writer Tolkien in his book *Lord of the Rings* suggested that runes were implements of power. It is true that they are an ancient and powerful tool, subject to a lot of folklore with a mystery of their own, but they should not be feared; rather they should be respected and cared for, in the same way as those students of the Tarot or crystals will care for their cards or gemstones, thanking them for their help and ensuring that they are looked after properly.

USING RUNES

Runes can be used in various ways – for example cast onto a cloth or other flat surface to provide a 'reading' in the same way as the Tarot or crystals, used as a means of altering the existing Western alphabet to provide alternative lettering for our names, and used in amulets. They can also be used for name changes, for those people who feel their existing name may have negative vibrations. Runes have been used in talismans and amulets, engraved on shields and swords and used for protection, healing and help since early times.

Those who are interested in changing names may also like to read *Numerology for Beginners*, another title in this series. It may also be of interest to followers of numerology that the numbers 3 and 8 were considered by the Vikings to have magical properties – but more of that later.

RUNIC LINKS

It is important to remember that runes are both an alphabetical system and a tool for self-help. Runes also link to the astrological elements of earth, air, fire and water, and are said by some modern runemasters to link with symbols of love. A glance at the symbols used on the runes will show that some of the signs seem to resemble the glyphs, or symbols, for the signs of the zodiac, and it is fair to say that the runes correspond easily to the planets. All these ways of using runes will be discussed as we progress.

Runes have strong links with both the Tarot and I Ching, which are the subject of other books in this series. The connections with the Tarot will be listed with each runic symbol from Chapter 4 onwards. The I Ching link relates to the polarity of the symbols, which again will be discussed with each rune. Whilst runes may be an ancient system, they are not archaic or outmoded and have as much relevance today as they ever did. The runic alphabet (see Figure 1.1) also relates to the system of numerology, as with most alphabetical systems, and also has colour links.

Figure 1.1   *The Elder Futhark*

The runic alphabet — saga and historical fact

Runic is an alphabet, a means of communication, and a set of symbols carved onto objects for magical purposes.

Nobody is totally certain where runes originated, or what the word 'rune' means. Whilst most runemasters suggest that the name means 'mystery' or 'holy secret', it is also worth considering that it may come from the German *raunen*, a word which has a variety of meanings, including 'to cut or carve'. Runes were most probably cut or carved and not written by the Norse who used them in ancient times. Other students of language suggest a link with the Anglo-Saxon word *secgan*, 'to say', and the Latin *secare*, 'to cut', whilst others suggest a link with the Old Nordic *run*, the Gothic *runa* and the Icelandic *runar*, all of which mean 'whisper'.

What is obvious from looking at the runes is that they are a series of straight lines with no curves or ellipses, which could obviously fit in with the idea of something carved by early man with basic implements. It is worth remembering that only educated people were taught to write or carve, and therefore those who could understand runes or carve them were people with extreme power.

There are several schools of thought on the origin of runes. Folklore suggests that they are older than the New Testament, and link with the one-eyed Norse god Odin (sometimes also called Woden the Wise). Odin was also called 'the shape-shifter' and had many guises. He sometimes hid the fact that he had one eye by wearing a large hat with the brim lowered. It is said that he gave his eye in exchange for being allowed to drink from the Well of Wisdom, hence his abundant knowledge. He is usually depicted with hat, blue cloak and staff, accompanied by two ravens, known as Hugin (Mind) and Munin (Memory), who kept him informed of what was happening.

Odin, a word which comes from the old Norse *od*, meaning 'spirit', is the Norse equivalent of the Roman Mercury, the Greek Hermes and the Egyptian Thoth. It is also interesting to note that spirit tracks (identified as ley lines in modern times) were considered sacred to Odin, so these, too, would seem to have a strong runic connection.

The story goes that Odin, wanting to understand life and death and needing to obtain wisdom, wounded himself with his own sword, with which he then impaled himself on a tree known as Yggdrasil, the Tree of the World or World Ash. He stayed there for nine days and nine nights without food, water or aid. Eventually he found enlightenment, fell, saw the runes and seized them. Later he wrote the Poetic Edda or Elder Edda, comprising 39 poems, in their honour. It is interesting to compare this story with the illustration on the Tarot card 'The Hanged Man'.

There are three main runic poems, Anglo-Saxon, Norwegian and Icelandic, mainly from the thirteenth and fifteenth centuries, and the Norse sagas contain many references to runes, their magic and power. The runic poems are important to the meanings of the runes, and all poems will be quoted as we progress.

Odin is seen by many runemasters as an essential part of working with runes. We will discuss Odin, and other gods, in more detail in Chapter 3.

Other versions of the origin of the runes are more historical, and are often favoured by those who merely look at the runes as a history of language. The runes commonly used now contain 24 characters,

plus a blank rune, fitting in with the Greek alphabet. It is said by many that the runic script was chiefly adapted from the Latin alphabet, but again this cannot be proven, and the characters used have not always numbered 24.

During the last Ice Age a tribe known as Volsungr, who were wanderers, used a system of wisdom known as Ur-Runes, which was said to give them certain powers. Moving down from the far north into Sweden, using a pathway called 'White Wyrm', they left behind examples of Ur-Runes in the Hallristningar rock carvings, dated between the second Iron Age and Bronze Age. Most runic inscriptions at that time were carved into rock, but this eventually changed as smaller stones, slivers of wood or bone as well as clay and metal were inscribed with runic characters. Unfortunately, few wooden runic crosses have survived.

Tribes moving further south carried runic knowledge towards what is now known as Austria, and in the fifth century BC, new alphabets were formulated, known now as North Etruscan, Alpine or North Italic. The Heruli warrior tribe became strongly identified with the runes and the name Herulian or Erilar became a common term for runemaster, long after the tribe had ceased to exist.

The Ur-Rune alphabet and the new Alpine alphabets at this point seem to merge. We are now at around 3 BC. Evidence of this exists in the Alpine text inscribed on a bronze helmet found at Negau, south of the Danube and dated at 3 BC.

The path of the runes then moved northwards down the Rhine, and there is evidence to suggest that the journey had reached the lower Rhine by around 1 BC. A first-century goblet on which runic symbols are etched has been found in the lower Rhine area. The journey continued along to the Friesian Islands (when possibly a further four new runes were added) then northwards into Denmark and Jutland and into Norway around AD 3, moving further north during the eighth and ninth centuries. The inscription on a fibula in Norway which has been dated AD 800, gives evidence that the Norse runic alphabet was being used at that time. There is evidence to suggest that the Futhark order of runes existed at this time but that the 24-character alphabet was not fixed.

When the Angles, Saxons and Jutes came to Britain, the alphabet increased to 29 runes, increasing in Northumbria during the early part of the ninth century to 33, possibly because more characters were needed to cope with the English phonetic system (as also in Germany), whilst in Denmark at the same time, 16 were used. A later progression saw 25 runes used in Scandinavia. The Northumbrian and Anglo-Saxon runes seemed to disappear for a time, but they reappeared in a 16-rune form during the time of the Norse and Danish invasions.

Examples of runic script in England can be found on the Bewcastle, Leek and Ruthwell crosses. The inscription on the Ruthwell Cross is the longest in the UK, and is located in the church in Ruthwell, Dumfriesshire. There are other runic inscriptions on a cross fragment in Lancaster and on a fragment at Thornhill in West Yorkshire. Runic was also used on some coins, as examples have survived with the names of kings written in runes. A visit to the British Museum to see Frank's Casket is well worth while, as it is probably the best-known of England's runic objects and the most studied. The runic script ceased to be commonplace in England following the arrival of Christian missionaries from Ireland, who introduced the roman alphabet to the masses. For a time, the runic script was still used for reference marks and as ornamental capitals, but this was fairly short-lived.

In the Middle Ages, a system comprising 25 runes was used in Sweden, and this is the system often found on Swedish runestones or standing stones.

As we have seen, the Vikings travelled far and wide and it has been suggested that there were even examples of eleventh-century Norse runestones as far away as the USA. This, however, has been disproven. The so-called Kensington Stone which can be found in Alexandria, Minnesota has been the subject of much discussion since its discovery in 1898. Current thought is that it is a fake, since the inscriptions on it seem to be a mixture of modern Swedish, Norwegian, Danish and English. It was hoped by the North Americans that the Vinland of the Norse sagas, actual location unknown, was somewhere on the North American coast. That may still be proven, but what is clear is that the Kensington Stone is

really nothing to do with the Vikings or genuine runic artefacts, and that most North American runic connections are still to be authenticated by archaeologists. It is possible in some cases that the objects found may be Eskimo in origin.

As suggested earlier, runes were probably not written down, but carved or etched on wood, metal, bone or stone. Only those who understood them learnt of their powers, and those who could decipher them were few and far between. As such, these people were often figures of authority who seemed to the masses to possess magical powers, being on a social level well above those unable to understand the symbols. Later on, the art of writing was reserved for the priesthood, for those connected with political matters, and for the nobility. Runes represented not only a method of communication or mnemonics but also symbols of knowledge.

During the seventeenth century there were serious attempts to ban the use of runes in Iceland, as the Church felt that there was a strong connection between runic writing, witchcraft and paganism. Records indicate that people were burnt to death in Iceland for merely possessing rune-staves. Likewise a ban was placed on the Bobileth tree writing, where every letter was named after a tree. Runic lettering had its supporters, however, one being Johannes Bureus, who sought to have the runes adopted as the official alphabet of Sweden in 1611, and runic calendars were still in use in some of the less populated areas of Sweden as late as the nineteenth century.

There are strong links between the runic alphabet and the Ogham alphabet of Wales and Ireland (discussed in depth later), and the Ogham script was one form of communication which was banned around the seventeenth century.

An interest in runes during the nineteenth century saw the creation of a new German system, known as the Armanen (see Figure 1.2), which has 18 characters. This was the 'brainchild' of Guido von List, and formed the basis of Nazi runelore. However, most runemasters used the 24 runes known as the Elder Futhark (also seen as *futhorc* or *fupark*), so called because of the order of the first six letters f, u, th, o, r and c.

Figure 1.2   *The Armanen 18 rune system*

During the twentieth century, interest in runes has revived, despite the stigma of Nazi usage, and the use of the SS during the time of Adolf Hitler of the double Sigel (also called Sol or Sygel) as their symbol, for political ends. However, this did not mean that students of the runes were exempt from persecution, and many runemasters and researchers were still persecuted. The association formed in the minds of many people between runes and the Nazi system meant that a true revival of runes did not begin until the late 1960s.

The Ogham script
connection

Several of the runestones still remaining have running around their edge a different alphabet from the runic, but one which still uses short, straight lines. This is the Ogham script (also seen as Ogam, but pronounced *O'am*).

Ogham is connected to the Celtic god Ogma, Ogmios or Ogmiua, who had connections with the sun. Whilst Odin seems to relate to Mercury, Ogma is linked with Hercules as champion of the gods.

Just as Odin is said to be the father of the runes, so Ogma is credited with having invented the Ogham script. This method of writing seems to have begun in Ireland, spreading to Wales, Scotland and parts of southern England.

Like Odin, Ogma was a poet and considered wise and powerful. Ogham was a secret method of communication, again only known by the learned. The connection with poetry has led Ogham to be termed 'the secret language of the poets'. To some, Ogma was merely a man, whilst to others he was a god. This is especially true in Ireland, where he is linked with the Tuatha de Danaan, the primal gods of Ireland.

The Ogham script has various styles and its ancient texts would seem to have contained information on early Druidism, forming a sacred system, as well as carrying coded messages which only the privileged understood. Sometimes the Ogham script was carved around the edge of a stone in order to immortalise a hero, whilst at other times it seems to have been used purely to mark boundaries.

It is certain that the Druids used the Ogham letters, and again it is interesting to note that Druidic teachings of that time were oral, like those of the Kabbala and of the runic alphabet.

Each of the 20 letters of the Ogham alphabet was linked with an element of nature, and some researchers suggest that each letter was linked with a tree (like the Bobileth to some degree), with each tree further associated with mythological tales and belief systems. Furthermore, certain trees were supposed to have links with particular months and the rites and rituals practised during that month. In much the same way, as we will discover, runic symbols were also often connected with plant, animal, bird and tree. The Ogham letters corresponded to several trees also used within the runic system.

The Ogham alphabet was arranged in groups of five, which contrasts with the runic Futhark, which is arranged in families of eight, with the blank rune remaining outside the 'family' group. The carvings were straight lines, as with runes, but above, below or through a central line, known as the *druim*. It was written from left to right.

In the same way that the runes were cast to seek help for a questioner, the Ogham script was used on branches or twigs, which were cast onto the ground, a process called *Crannchur* (casting the woods) and 'read'. Other methods included the use of wooden dice, which were thrown in a similar way to modern dice. Thus the

Ogham script not only became a means of communication but also took on magical properties, being used for the writing of spells and charms and engraved on amulets and talismans, and considered as magic in itself. Those who have studied its form suggest it was probably the most powerful alphabet of them all.

Owing to feelings within the early Christian Church that such alphabets were evil, connected with paganism and witchcraft, the Ogham script was banned, and has to all extents and purposes disappeared in modern usage, which is a shame, except for those who have made it their life's work to research and rediscover it.

Consulting the runes

The runes can be consulted in many ways, principally, however, by casting them. It is said, as we have already briefly mentioned, that they can also be used for protection, in matters of health and finance, and we will discuss these suggestions briefly before moving on to the most common usage of runes. The lettering used for such matters will be discussed as we progress through the alphabetical system.

Protection

Viking legend suggests that runes were buried around items needing protection from wandering tribes likely to rape and pillage, as well as being used for the protection of women and children whilst the Vikings were away.

I have heard of people leaving runes to care for their property whilst going on holiday – with some success. Some have hewn runic symbols above their front door for protection, whilst others have even used runic symbolism to protect their car from theft. In Viking times, runic symbols were often carved on the stern of longboats to offer protection. These were known to the Vikings as Brun runes.

Healing

Vikings used runes for healing and this tradition continues today. Those who study runes often carry them on visits to hospital or to the doctor, or in exam situations, just as students of crystals carry gemstones. Healing runes were known as Lim runes, and the symbols were carved into the south-facing bark or leaves of appropriate healing trees.

Below is a list of runes, together with the help they reputedly offer to various parts of the body. I have not personally tried runes for healing, but can see no reason why they should not be tried out by those wishing to do so. However, irrespective of whether you are using runes, crystals, herbs or whatever, please do not abandon medication prescribed to you by your doctor. All these forms of healing should be viewed as complementary rather than alternatives to orthodox medication. Seek proper medical help and use things like runes as a 'top-up'.

I suggest that you try meditating with the rune connected to the particular complaint. You might also try using the symbol of the rune in an item of jewellery which you carry with you permanently, to reinforce any healing.

Fehu	Chest and respiratory problems
Uruz	Muscles and anything connected with bodily strength
Thurisaz	Heart
Ansuz	Mouth, teeth, throat, stutters
Raido	Legs and gluteal muscles
Kaunaz	Cysts, ulcers, abscesses and boils and any fever associated
Gebo	Toxic poisoning
Wunjo	Breathing problems
Hagalaz	Wounds, grazes, cuts

Nauthiz	The arms
Isa	Any loss of feeling or sensation
Jera	Bowel or digestive disorders
Eihwaz	Eye problems
Perth	Anything associated with childbirth or sexual organs
Algiz	Mental or anxiety problems, head or brain, headaches
Sowelu	Burns or skin problems
Teiwaz	Rheumatics and arthritis, especially of hands
Berkana	Fertility problems
Ehwaz	Anything associated with the back
Mannaz	Sprains, pulled tendons, etc., especially of feet or ankles
Laguz	Kidneys
Inguz	Problems associated with male genitalia
Othila	Genetic problems, anything inherited
Dagaz	Fear, distress, nervous problems, mental illness

Money

Unlike the ancients, modern man has much need of money. Its acquisition seems to be a powerful force which drives many men to greed and avarice, as well as to ill health. However, it is said that you can obtain financial help through using the runes, provided that the need is genuine and necessary and not just adding to already bulging coffers! If intending to use runes for financial matters, make sure you think long and hard about the need behind the desire, and not just of the desire itself, and also be prepared to receive the money in ways other than those envisaged. Remember - the money must be needed for necessities and must be an essential, not just an added bonus. The acquisition of money can come through using the

runic letters to form a word, or by the use of the numbers 3 and 8, both of which were felt by the Vikings to have strong powers, or multiples thereof.

Runes and meditation

Those who wish to meditate with runes may find they are particularly enlightening when used either individually, or in words formed for particular purposes, such as healing.

Meditation can be a particularly healing process. It can help you to focus your mind on something outside your daily life, and it can help to calm and compose you. I feel it is important to take time out as often as possible to get back in touch with yourself, and meditation can be an ideal vehicle, for this.

You may also wish to meditate further on the meaning of the runes. One way of doing this is to sit with the rune, away from telephones, children, TV and other distractions, and begin to meditate by concentrating on slow breathing. Closing your eyes, try to keep the symbol of the rune in your mind's eye and see what comes to you.

There are many ways of meditating, and it is important that you find the best way for you personally. Experienced meditators will find no problem using runes in their meditation. Others might need several attempts before feeling comfortable with this.

Viking uses for the runes

As mentioned earlier, the Vikings used runes for a variety of purposes. When used magically they were known as Ram runes. We have already seen how Lim and Brun runes were used, and that they can still be used in this way today. In addition, there were other titles for runes used for magical purposes. Used for 'righting wrongs', Mal or speech runes were often etched in or around areas used for trials. Sig runes, on the other hand, were used to win battles and contests, and were etched on a warrior's weapons and armour to bring about success.

It is said that rune chants were used for the conception, gestation and birth of a child, and at birth, runes were cast to find the name and life-path of the baby. Runes used for protection at birth were known as Biarg runes, while Swart runes were used after a death in an effort to help the departed spirit return to its ancestors. In addition, Hug runes were used to confer mental agility. Legend also suggests that runes were used for incidental things, like trying to attract the attention and subsequent love of a maiden, and for purposes of enchantment.

Finally, runes were often used by healers to help decide what herbs and potions to use on the sick.

Casting the runes

Each individual will eventually devise his or her own way of casting the runes. What follows are some suggestions, all following a similar path, but they are by no means fixed rules. We will discuss ways of casting the runes in Chapter 7.

It is important to remember that your runes are your own, and are special. You have created a link with them and that is important. Never lend your runes, unless you feel comfortable doing this. I personally would never lend runes, Tarot cards or crystals to anyone else. If you are unsure, maybe you should try drawing a rune from your pouch and seeing what you get as an answer. It is suggested that an upright rune gives a Yes answer, and an inverted one a No answer. However, those runes which look the same either way may prove a problem!

A traditional way of casting the runes is to mix them in a pouch and cast them on a cloth, usually velvet. I keep my runes in such a pouch and use them in this way. It usually happens that the runes I am intended to use find their way into my hand or between my fingers as I mix them in the pouch. I usually draw nine runes.

Others have suggested drawing three runes at a time, three times, with a break in between each set of three.

Old Nordic tales suggest that throwing runes at a person was a means of casting a magical spell. Likewise spells are said to have been cast by writing certain runic inscriptions on a piece of paper and passing it to the unsuspecting intended victim.

All these things may belong in folklore, and have no bearing on the modern usage for runes; it is up to the individual to decide. One runemaster I know draws three runes which represent current circumstances. Having looked at these three runes, he returns them to the pouch and draws three more. The second set of three represents courses of action or possible outcomes. The second set is then also returned to the pouch and a final single rune drawn, which indicates influences likely to have a bearing on the problem as a whole.

Tradition suggests that Odin's number was 5. For this reason, some runemasters work with only five runes. Those interested in numerology will note that the runes total 25 if you include the blank rune. This all adds up to 7, which is a powerful and spiritual number, and for this reason, perhaps, some runemasters draw seven runes when casting.

Another means of casting the runes is to 'shuffle them' and leave them to their own devices for a while (15 minutes is usually suggested), and then draw 12, laying them on a horoscope chart especially prepared for the purpose.

We have now briefly introduced ourselves to the runes, and are more aware of their foundation and usage. As already stated, more detailed descriptions of casting the runes will be given at a later stage.

Before we are able to discuss each rune in sequence, we will look at the sort of runes to buy, and whether it is better to make your own set, and at the symbols.

However, before we go on, let's have a quick quiz on what we have learnt so far.

PRACTICE

Don't panic – this isn't an exam, but it could serve to focus your attention on runes a little more closely. All the answers can be found in the text, and no answers are given here, so it's up to you to find your own solutions.

- Who was Odin?

- All original runes were carved on wood. True or false?

- The Elder Futhark system uses 20 runes plus a blank rune. True or false?

- The Ogham script is another Scandinavian alphabetical system. True or false?

- Odin and Ogma are one and the same person. True or false?

- The Nazis used a runic symbol in its double form during the Second World War. Which symbol was used?

THREE FAMILIES IN ONE

*I*t is important to introduce the runes as a group before delving into the details of each rune and its meanings.

Runes are symbols connecting man with his unconscious or spirit, and each rune has its own links and its own meanings, both in upright and reversed position, in much the same way as do the Tarot cards. There will be much to learn about each rune; not only its meanings but its ancient English and Germanic names.

However, before we do that, we should discuss what sort of runes to purchase, and whether it is advisable and indeed practical to make your own runes.

WHAT RUNES TO BUY

Ideally runes should be made of wood or stone. Other natural substances can be used, and I know of runemasters using limestone, slate and bone. The set I have are stones on which are etched the symbols of each rune.

Runes can normally be bought in New Age shops, by mail order and occasionally in gift shops. Make sure you look around at all that is available and feel comfortable with the set you intend to buy. It is most important that you feel the runes before purchase. If this proves a problem due to packaging, explain your need to the retailer, as I am sure they will understand. It is not unusual, and it is in fact similar to people buying Tarot cards wanting to look through the illustrations and feel the cards before purchase.

Making your own runes

Before deciding what to make your runes out of, it is worth considering which alphabetical system to use. These follow several forms, but most runes will use the common German Futhark symbols used in this book. However, if you feel you have an affinity with ancient English, a little alteration will produce slightly different symbols. As you learn more about runes and read more about their usage, you may find that you end up with several sets of runes, all using different symbolism. Make sure, however, that you keep each set of runes separate and do not mix the systems.

There are many substances you can choose to make your own runes. If you want to make them out of pebbles, try to ensure that the pebbles are similar in size, and be very careful to copy the symbols exactly if endeavouring to paint them yourself. Also make sure that you use a paint which will not flake or fade, preferably made from a natural pigment. It is said that the Vikings often used blood to stain their runes; I wouldn't recommend this, but I would suggest that a red pigment is used, red having a strong association with the god Thor. Those who wish to use the colour associated with Odin should use blue. Traditionally it is suggested that the pebbles used should be gathered from the seashore during a storm, so bear this in mind should you live near or be visiting the seaside!

People who are keen on pottery or have access to a kiln may like to try to make their runes out of clay or ceramics. Another possibility is making a set out of card. This is especially useful as a starting set, or if money is scarce. Each runic card should be around 1" wide by 2" long at least.

Those who are able to carve might like trying to make a set of runes out of one of the traditional woods, such as hazel, birch, ash or apple. Ash is a strongly runic tree, being the tree in which Odin hung, and birch is also a wood traditionally used for rune-making. Apple wood is often used because of the connection with the Goddess Idun, who kept apples in a basket which, it is said, kept age at bay. Some runemasters suggest that it is acceptable to make runes out of yew, but others suggest that, to the Vikings, the yew was a tree of death, and so should not be used. This stems from the fact that its bark, leaves, roots and fruit are all poisonous. However, it can also be seen as the tree of life, as it stays green throughout the year, and can be regenerated by its own daughter-tree growing in the soil inside the dying trunk. It is therefore up to the individual to decide whether to use yew or not.

Tradition suggests that such wood should be cut from a tree during the waning of the moon, and chopped into the 25 pieces immediately. It is important to ask permission of the tree before doing this, explaining the purpose behind your action. The tree is a living thing and should be treated with respect. It is of course equally important that you ask permission of the tree's owner, should it not be in your own garden! Some traditions also suggest that you should leave a silver coin somewhere within the tree for payment, but this is up to the individual concerned.

Each piece should be flattened and smoothed before the symbols are carved, and sharp tools used. Any paint put onto the carving to darken or further distinguish the symbols should be made from a natural pigment. Another way of marking the runes could be burning the letters, but this should be done with care and by someone who knows exactly what they are doing. Likewise it is important to be fairly confident, when making your own runes out of wood, firstly that you have enough wood for the job, and secondly that you are capable of the task.

As it is said that Wednesday connects with Odin (Woden's day – Woden being another form of Odin), you may decide to embark upon making your runes on that day.

Cleansing and protecting the runes

As with crystals, runes should be cleaned, especially if they are bought from a commercial outlet. They should be washed in natural water, preferably spring water, or at least mineral water (check the label to make sure that it has not been irradiated), and left to dry before being put into a pouch or bag, which traditionally should be leather, felt, silk or velvet. A pouch with a drawstring is ideal. Tradition suggests that the drawstring or thong should be leather, but those people who are against using animal products may think otherwise.

Some people who have made their own runes out of wood like to keep them in a box made of the same wood from the same tree. Again, this is a matter of personal preference. Many runemasters also use a casting cloth, onto which the runes are cast. This is another matter of personal choice, but it is worth noting that a casting cloth will help to prevent damage to the runes and keep them clean.

Introducing the Aetts

In the Elder Futhark, in other words the 24-plus-one runic set with which we are concerned here, there are three divisions. These divisions contain eight runes each, the blank or 25th rune being a separate item. This is similar to the Greek division of the alphabet into three ogdoads (groups of eight), said to reflect the three parts of the universe. Each of these sets has its own name, and is called an *aett*, an Icelandic word, with many meanings included in which are things connected with place, lineage and eight directions. It is interesting to note that the Scottish word *airt* is very similar, as is the Irish word *aird* meaning an eighth of the horizon, and used as a means of direction. The number eight is said to have been a very powerful number to the Vikings and each set of eight runes forms its own 'family', and is assigned to a particular god.

There are three sets of aetts, three being another particularly powerful number to the Vikings. The first set is called Freyr's aett, the second set Haegl's aett (the ninth rune itself is called Haegl), and the third set Tyr's aett (the 17th rune itself is called Tyr or Tiw). You may also see the word *aettir* used instead of *aett*. It is important to realise that, whilst each runic set has its god, the overall ruler of the runes remains Odin, rather than those mentioned above.

Freyr's set is said to represent growth, increase and unfolding, Haegl's set the elements, and Tyr's set courage in the face of adversity, Tyr being a warrior god. In addition to each set being assigned a particular god, many of the individual runes were also assigned a god. These will be given when we discuss each rune individually, along with details of the planet or zodiac sign connected with each rune, and other connections, such as animal or nature associations. In this chapter, however, we will go so far as to link four of the runes with the elements of earth, air, fire and water, considering how other runes may also link with the elements, and also briefly consider a feminist connection.

I would point out at this stage that the Nordic races had little connection with the zodiac, and so linking runes to zodiac signs is a relatively modern idea.

Each aett is set out in sequence, from right to left, with Freyr's aett being the top row, and so on. Many runemasters will lay out the runes in these lines before use, feeling that this imprints the runes with their personal vibration, afterwards collecting them and putting them into their pouch.

Alphabetical and Language Links

We know already that each runic symbol represents a mnemonic. Each symbol also represents a letter. Each symbol can be shown in modern English lettering, Old English lettering or German lettering, as well as in Norwegian and Icelandic symbols. It is not vital to know all these connections, but it is important to be able to see that there are other symbols for the runes, as you may well buy or wish to make a set with slightly different symbols from the modern English with which we will principally deal here, especially if you have an interest in personalising your own runes or have a particular historical interest. In addition to each symbol in the languages mentioned, each rune has a name in that language, which will be given in a separate list.

Please note that some runemasters transpose the 23rd and 24th rune. In other words, you will sometimes find that Dagaz comes before Othila, rather than as shown here, which is considered by many to be the traditional order.

The Germanic letterings given will correspond to the runic symbol normally used.

RUNIC SYMBOLS

Modern	Old English	Germanic	Norwegian	Icelandic
F	ᚨ	ᚠ	ᚠ	ᚠ
U or W	ᚱ	ᚱ	ᚱ	ᚱ
TH or P	ᚦ	ᚦ	ᚦ	ᚦ
A or O	ᚫ	ᚠ	ᚨ	ᚨ
R	ᚱ	ᚱ	ᚱ	ᚱ
K or C	ᚻ	ᚲ	ᛉ	ᛉ
G	ᚷ	ᚷ	-	-
W, U or V	ᚹ	ᚹ	-	-
H	ᚾ	ᚾ or ᚺ	ᚼ	ᚼ

Modern	Old English	Germanic	Norwegian	Icelandic
N				
I				
J, G or Y				
E, EO or EI			–	–
P			–	–
Z, E or Y			–	–
S				
T				
B				
E				
M				
L				
NG			–	–

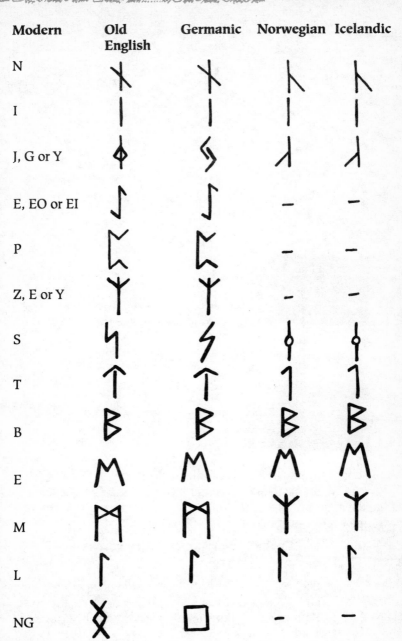

Modern	Old English	Germanic	Norwegian	Icelandic
O or E	ᛟ	ᛟ	–	–
D	ᛞ	ᛞ	–	–
A	ᚪ	–	–	–
AE	ᚫ	–	–	–
Y	ᛨ	–	–	–
IO	ᛦ	–	–	–
EA	ᛠ	–	–	–
Y	–	–	ᛣ	↕

RUNIC NAMES

We are concentrating here only on the Anglo-Saxon or Old English and on the Germanic. Norwegian and Icelandic names are given during the course of the quotation of their respective poems, before each rune is discussed in detail.

English letter	Old English name	Germanic name	Keywords
F	Feoh	Fehu	Cattle/prosperity
U or W	Ur	Uruz	Wild ox/strength
TH or P	Porn or Thorn	Purisaz	Thorn/defence/giant

English letter	Old English name	Germanic name	Keywords
A or O	Os	Ansuz	
		Asa	God Odin/holy power
R	Rad	Raido	Wheel/motion/travel
K or C	Cen or Cean	Kaunaz	
		Kenaz	Bonfire/illumination
		Kano	
G	Gyfu	Gebo	Gift/partnership
W, U or V	Wyn	Wunjo	Joy/happiness
H	Haegl	Hagalaz	Hail/constraint
N	Nyd	Nauthiz	Need/necessity
I	Is	Isa	Ice/standstill
J, G or Y	Ger	Jera	Harvest/year/cycle
E, EO or EI	Eoh	Eihwaz	Yewtree/defence
P	Peord	Perth	Initiation/womb
Z, E or Y	Eolh	Algiz	Reed/guardianship
S	Sigel	Sowelu	Sun/life force
T	Tir	Teiwaz	Wargod Tyr or Tir
B	Beorc	Berkana	Birchtree/growth
E	Eh	Ehwaz	Horse/movement
M	Man	Mannaz	Human being
L	Lagu	Laguz	Lake/fluidity/flow
NG	Ing	Inguz	Male fertility/energy
O or E	Epel or Ethel	Othila	Inheritance/home
D	Daeg	Dagaz	Day/breakthrough
A	Ac	–	Oaktree
AE	Aesc	–	Ashtree
Y	Yr	–	Horn
IO	Iar or Ior	–	Eel
EA	Ear	–	Grave/death

Before we progress to looking at each rune in isolation, perhaps we should consider another connection with runes – that of the elements. Whilst Vikings, as we have said, had little or no connections with astrology and the zodiac, they were very aware of the elements, and there is no reason to suppose that the elemental links are totally modern in concept. Indeed the runes are founded on the differences between fire and ice.

Elemental Links

Most people with even a smattering of knowledge of astrology will be aware of the elements of earth, air, fire and water, and that three zodiac signs fit into each element. It should come as no surprise, therefore, to learn that a rune also corresponds to each element.

What follows here are the most widely accepted linkages between the elements and four of the runes. Also given are other runes which are said to link in with the element being discussed.

Earth

The element of earth is concerned with solid foundations, and with keeping in touch with reality. It may be interesting to learn that Eihwaz, an earth rune, is sometimes called 'the Rune of Death' because of the poisonous qualities of the yew tree with which it is associated.

Also associated with the earth element are Uruz, Wunjo, Berkana, Othila, Isa (which can also link with the water element, ice being frozen water) and Jera. Isa, Eihwaz and Jera are also said to link with the New Moon.

Water

Kaunaz is, surprisingly, a water rune. It relates to bonfires, but does not equate to the element of fire. To the Vikings, bonfires were a physical light in the darkness, as well as symbolising inner knowledge or enlightenment. It relates to emotions and intuition, and therefore its element is water. Some runemasters will disagree here, preferring to keep Kaunaz with its symbol of fire.

Also associated with the water element are Perth, Lagu, Ing, Raido and Gebo. Hagalaz has connections with ice, and so also correctly belongs with this element. Kaunaz, Raido and Gebo are said to link with the waning of the moon. Gebo and Raido also link with the element of air.

AIR

Ansuz, an air rune has a strong connection with Odin, who was considered to have discovered the runes in the root of the Tree of the World, and as such has a link with the ash tree. He was also considered to be the source of knowledge and inspiration and it therefore follows that Odin should be described as the source of language, and the runes as a form of communication. Ansuz relates to the element of air, to divine breath, to thought and to the power of the intellect.

Also associated with the element of air are Teiwaz, Berkana (which also links to earth having a duality in element) and Ehwaz, which also link with the waxing of the moon. Algiz is also said to link with the air element, as do Sowelu and Mannaz.

It should be noted that some runemasters suggest that Ansuz is more correctly linked with fire and water rather than air.

FIRE

Dagaz is a fire rune, and represents day, breakthrough. It is associated, too, with the dawn of the world, since the earth was born in flames. Dagaz is considered to be the illuminator, the light, and as such cannot be destroyed. It is the guardian by the doorway, a protective force against anything harmful. Dagaz is another case of elemental duality, associated both with fire and air.

Also associated with the element of fire are Othila and Fehu, which also link with the full moon, and with the element of earth – again, being dual in elemental nature. Thurisaz, Nauthiz and Eihwaz are also said to link with fire, but it is worth noting that many runemasters consider Eihwaz as belonging to all elements.

The FEMINIST CONNECTION

Feminism is often wrongly considered to be a modern concept. In ancient cultures there often existed a strong 'goddess orientation', and despite rather than because of the women's movement worldwide, there has over recent years been a huge revival of interest in 'goddess-oriented' matters.

Women were often considered as special by virtue of the fact that they often possessed powers, magical to some, healing to others, which placed them at a high level in society. They were not always the subordinates that they have subsequently been portrayed as.

Whilst it may be difficult to comprehend when thinking of the all-male image of the Viking warrior, there is none the less a strong feminist link with the runes.

We have already mentioned the fact that the knowledge of the runes was limited to a few people, normally those who were considered learned and wise. Amongst these were many women, who were often regarded as especially wise. Magical traditions in Scandinavia were mostly taught by women, and there is evidence to suggest that many women carved their own runes.

There were several female gods, including Freya, Frigg and Idun. It is worth noting that Freya was one of Odin's teachers and is often shown as a patroness of war, possibly like Boudicca. The rune Fehu is connected to Freya. Frigg also has her own rune, Wyn. Frigg was considered to be the Fairy Queen.

Other runes, too, are connected to women figures: Thurisaz with the goddess Thrud, whose name means power and strength; Ansuz with the goddess Asir; and Kaunaz with Freya, Snotra, Vor and Var, all goddesses of wisdom and learning. Gebo has connections with Gefn, goddess of the material life, Hagal with the goddess Hela, and Isa with Rinda, goddess of the frozen earth. Jera, being connected with fertility, links well with the goddesses of fertility, Freya and Frigg. Perth, one keyword for which is womb, has obvious feminine connections. Another of its keywords is sometimes given as 'holy pot', again with strong feminine connections. Sigel, whose other name is Sol (the sun) has connections with a goddess also called Sol, whilst Inguz has links with the Danish goddess Yngona, the symbol for Inguz having been found on stones within Denmark. Othila, also seen as Ethel, again has obvious feminine links and is said to be the rune of Erda, whilst Dagaz links with the goddess Syn,

guardian of the door, which fits with Dagaz's associations with breakthrough and day.

We have now formally introduced the runes as a whole and must start to look at them individually before learning how they create a picture when cast.

Before moving on, however, we mustn't forget our quiz. Again, the answers are somewhere within the chapter for you to find, and will not be given here.

PRACTICE

- Which rune has 'ox' as one of its keywords?

- Odin is connected with the rune called Sigel. True or false?

- Everyone agrees that the final rune before the blank rune is the rune called Daeg. True or false?

- Why do some runemasters suggest that you should not make your runes out of yew?

- Which rune has 'ice' as one of its keywords?

- What other names can the rune called Cen be known by?

3 GODS AND POETRY

*I*n order to familiarise yourself with the runes, you need to have your own set at this stage. If you have not had time to purchase a set or have not yet found one to your liking, consider making a temporary set out of card.

However, before we start to look at the runes in detail, we must look at the main Viking gods, familiarise ourselves a little with them, their alleged powers and also their names, as runes often relate to a specific god.

The Viking gods

There were three main Norse gods – Odin, Freyr and Thor. However, that was not always the case. Evidence suggests that Odin, whose name is so strongly linked with the runes, was not always the principal god, the All-Father or sky god. The original holder of this position was a god called Tyr, Tiew, Ziu, Tiwaz or Teiwaz. He is linked to his own rune, as we will shortly see, as well as to the third aett named after him, and his name was often engraved on the bracelets of warriors to protect them in battle. You may come across him linked with the goddess Zisa, who was his consort.

Tyr was the Norse equivalent of the roman god Zeus, and his following was particularly strong in Denmark. He was a god of war, was considered exceptionally powerful and courageous, and it is said lost his right hand in a battle with a wolf. He was, therefore, frequently known as 'the one-handed god'. Odin, it is said, superseded Tyr.

Odin was a god of mystery and disguise, and of deep power. He often disguised himself to travel around the world, and was a sinister figure rather than an attractive one. To the Anglo-Saxons, Odin became Woden, which was said to mean 'fury', but it is said that he had up to 170 other names, all reflecting his complex personality, one of which was 'Lord of the Slain'. Sometimes you may come across the name Thund. This is yet another name for Odin, as is All-Father.

It is said that within his heaven, or Asgard, was Odin's palace, called Valhöll (or more usually in English Valhalla), the Hall of the Slain, where fallen warriors went after their death to feast and prepare for the Last Battle which would mean the doom of the Gods, or Ragnarok. Valhöll, it is said, was a huge palace, containing around 640 doorways, through which 960 warriors could march shoulder to shoulder. Legend suggests that the runes, which Odin seized having suspended himself on the tree Yggdrasil, were representative of the magical knowledge which could only be obtained from the dead.

Creatures with strong connections with Odin were the wolf, the eagle and the raven. A wolf was said to lurk near the western door of Valhöll, whilst an eagle hovered overhead. The ravens stayed with Odin, apart from flying round the world on his request to see what could be spied. In addition to the wolf guarding a doorway to Valhöll, Odin was said to have two pet wolves, to whom he gave all his food, preferring to receive all his nourishment from wine.

Odin was considered god of the dead, of warriors, war and magic, and the patron of poetry. His spear, Gungnir, was always with him, and he is often shown with his horse, Sleipnir, an animal with eight legs. He was frequently found with an old blue cloak, a wide-brimmed hat pulled over one eye, and his ravens for company. He had a wife called Frigg (commemorated in the word Friday or Frigg's day), and two sons, Thor and Baldur. Thor, however, was far more powerful.

Thor is Odin's most well-known son. He is shown as a huge red-haired man, with red beard and red eyes, waving a hammer, known as Mjolnir, with which he protected the world. The hammer could be thrown or swung, and always returned to Thor's hand, in much the same way as a boomerang. He is sometimes known as the Lord Protector of the Universe, or God of Thunder, as he had under his power the elements of thunder and lightning. Thor spent his time in the heavens in his chariot drawn by two sacred goats, killing the giants who lived just outside the limits of civilisation, in an attempt to protect Asgard (heaven) and Midgard (the universe inhabited by man).

The Vikings believed that a storm resulted from Thor moving around heaven in his chariot, the thunder being evidence of his movement, the lightning of the throwing of his hammer.

Thor was the god of seamen and farmers, governing thunder and lightning, and wind and rain, as well as better weather. He was also guardian of the world, was powerful, brave and noble, and one to whom man and god alike turned in times of trouble. One of the runic symbols is said to represent Thor's hammer. His other treasured possessions are said to have been a magic belt and a pair of iron gauntlets.

There is a theory that Thor was as powerful a figure in Viking life as Odin – or more so – as Thor's temple was always given the prime spot.

The other important god to the Vikings was Freyr or Frey. Freyr and his twin sister Freya were linked with ancient gods concerned with the earth and associated with the seasons. Freyr was the god of fertility and of increase, associated strongly with the spring as well as the summer sunshine, and was considered to control both rainfall and sunshine. Freyr was not only a god of fertility but of peace as well as good fortune. The animal most sacred to Freyr was the wild boar, and he was considered the most important god of all to the Swedish. Legend says that Freyr's most treasured possession was his ship called Skiobladnir, built by dwarfs, like Thor's hammer, and large enough to carry all the gods. However, this large ship could be folded up and put in a pouch when not in use! Freyr's aett is dedicated to this god.

Other Viking gods included Njord, god of the sea, and father of Freyr and Freya, Heimdal, guardian of the bridge leading up to the

heavens, after which Hagal's aett is named, together with the underworld guardian goddess Mordgud, and Loki, brother to Odin and considered to be a trickster.

Runic meanings

Runes can have spiritual meanings in castings and other meanings based on their traditional foundations. These will be given, as will also the animal or nature connection, any zodiac connection and any planetary connection. Please remember, however, that the astrological connections are based on modern thinking, and are not traditional. We will be quoting from all three main runic poems and will also be giving details of the god associated with the rune under discussion. We will also link each rune with a Tarot card (using Thorsson's versions), a colour and a polarity. Meanings will be given for the rune in upright and reverse positions, but it is worth considering that not all runemasters use reverse meanings.

It is important that you consider any hidden or spiritual meaning when looking at the runes. Where the rune specifically calls for you to address this part of yourself, this will be clear in the text. However, don't assume that when no spiritual meaning is specified none exists. That may be for you to find alone. It may be necessary for you to meditate on this for yourself, or conversely call up any intuitive powers you have and formulate your own ideas. As you progress, you may discover that the runes have special personal meanings for you. All this will come with experience, and you must be patient.

Runic poetry

The names of the runes will follow the Germanic or Elder Futhark. As stated, we will be quoting from all the runic poetry. It is, however, important to realise that the Norwegian and Icelandic runic poems relate to the 16 runes used in that system, whereas the Anglo-Saxon runic poem covers 29 runes. We are only covering the

24 runes of the Elder Futhark. We will briefly discuss the remaining five Anglo-Saxon rune verses and symbols in Chapter 5, plus the others from the Norwegian and Icelandic poems which do not feature as part of the Elder Futhark. Other symbols for the runes will also be given where they are dramatically different from the Germanic symbol, but the names for the runes will be their Germanic ones.

PRACTICE

- Who were the three main Norse gods?
- Which three creatures were associated with Odin?
- How many runes are there in the Norwegian and Icelandic system?

FREYR'S AETT

*T*his chapter looks at Freyr's aett: Fehu, Uyuz, Thurisaz, Ansuz, Raitho and Kaunaz. As we saw in the last chapter, Freyr (or Frey) was a god of fertility, peace and good fortune.

FEHU

Zodiac sign Taurus   **Tarot link – The Tower**   **Colour – red**
Polarity – female

This rune is said to relate to the cat, the swallow and to the elder tree and nettle. The god linked to this rune is Freyr or Freyja.

The Anglo-Saxon runic poem reads: 'Feoh is comfort to all men, yet must everyman bestow it freely, if he wish to gain honour in the sight of the Great One.'

The Norwegian runic poem reads: 'Fe causes trouble among kinsmen; wolf dwells in forest.'

The Icelandic runic poem reads 'Fe is trouble among kinsmen and fire of sea and path of serpent.'

Fehu means possessions. To the Vikings, the ownership of cattle signified movable wealth, money and success. Regarded as status symbols, they implied that the owner had power and authority, and the potential to negotiate should he choose. In the modern world this is still the case in parts of Africa. Possessions can, remember, be either acquired, bought or gained. They need not necessarily come about as a result of hard work. Likewise it should be remembered that possessions need looking after, so an element of conservation is also involved here. Making money is one thing, but keeping it is quite another! That doesn't mean we should be greedy or envious of others with wealth, and the rune poems warn of this.

The rune calls for us to protect and take care of ourselves and our possessions. It also concerns the potential for wealth and possessions, and the need to consider sharing with others – being responsible if you like. It represents the foundations from which we all come, together with the ability to control others, ourselves and our circumstances.

Fehu is said to link with nourishment (the milk of the cow), well-being (the result of proper nourishment) and fertility (obviously connecting to childbirth and the production of milk). Being the first rune of Freyr's aett, this rune strongly connects to the god Freyr, sometimes seen as Frey, a god of fertility. To modern runemasters this rune is also therefore associated with love, although it does not form one of the four main 'Runes of Love' which will be discussed later. It can also indicate a possible pregnancy, or a new start in another direction.

IN REVERSE

Loss of something valuable is suggested here. This could be a material possession, or it could be a friendship or loved one. Perhaps any article lost is really only misplaced. Maybe possessions are not really necessary. There may be problems relating to procreation. This could suggest a fertility problem, but also a lack of creative stimulus.

URUZ

Planet Pluto   Tarot link – The High Priestess
Colour – green   Polarity – male

This rune relates to the wild ox or auroch, a creature of great strength. Aurochs, or Viking oxen, extinct since the seventeenth century, had long sharp horns, and therefore a connection with 'the horn of plenty' has been established. These animals were fast-moving and capable of transporting exceptionally heavy loads. This rune therefore suggests that a burden may be placed upon our shoulders with which we will be able to cope, despite doubts to the contrary. The god linked to this rune is Thor, the tree is the birch, and the plant Icelandic moss.

The Anglo-Saxon runic poem reads: 'Ur is proud and has great horns. It is a courageous beast and fights with its horns, a great ranger of moors, it is a creature of mettle.'

The Norwegian runic poem reads: 'Ur come from poor iron; reindeer runs oft over hard-frozen snow.' In this poem *Ur* means 'Slag'.

The Icelandic runic poem reads: 'Ur is weeping of clouds and destruction of hay-harvest and abhorrence of herdsmen.' In this poem 'Ur' means 'Drizzle'.

Oxen are essentially masculine, physical and strong. This rune therefore concerns matters of strength, and also of opportunities and power. This represents our own limitless power. However, as with any strong beast, the auroch cannot be pushed, so be careful how much force is used in any situation. This rune also concerns energy, and it is necessary to harness the energy in the best possible way in order to achieve a favourable outcome. Things are likely to change when this rune is drawn, but it is up to the individual to make the most of the ensuing changes. New beginnings often bring with them periods of uncertainty. Things may not always be what they seem. Sometimes it is necessary to take a risk. Things may not happen overnight, so be patient and don't give up.

This is a good rune to draw if you are expecting promotion or advancement. It is worth remembering that these meanings could concern someone other than yourself. The Vikings often used the auroch in sacrifices, and it is important to remember that there may be some element of sacrifice required when this rune is drawn.

IN REVERSE

Do not miss opportunities. Be aware that you may miss a chance to change your life. The connection with strength also suggests that there may be a physical or mental weakness, a short illness or lack of strength. This could be a good opportunity to review your diet, reduce stress, or even to take some extra vitamins!

THURISAZ

Planet Jupiter   Tarot link – The Emperor   Colour – red
Polarity – male

This rune also relates to the snake and to the blackthorn tree, as well as to the thorn of a bush or even of a rose. It is also said to connect to the houseleek.

The Anglo-Saxon runic poem reads: 'Thorn is exceeding sharp, a baneful thing for a warrior to touch, uncommonly severe on all who lie amongst them.'

The Norwegian runic poem reads: 'Purs causes illness in women; few rejoice at ill luck.' In this poem and the Icelandic poem, *Purs* means 'Giant'.

The Icelandic runic poem reads: 'Purs is illness of women and cliff dweller and husband of Varthrun.'

This rune has strong connections with the god Thor, an aggressive personality, and it therefore follows that this rune connects with defence, standing one's ground, with aggression and conflict. In Viking times, thickets of hawthorn or blackthorn were used to delineate a boundary which kept out intruders, and this defensive connection should also be remembered. These problems may be minor, but will cause worry. They can, however, be easily overcome in time.

This rune suggests that now is not the time to make hasty decisions, as things are likely to change without warning. This time should be used to look at what has been achieved and what is still to be achieved, and perhaps to let go of the past.

People may not be as sincere as you think, nor as reliable. In the same way that a rose looks beautiful, it is worth remembering that the thorn on the rose bush can cause a wound, either small or large.

Business dealings should be carefully watched. There may also be rivalries and jealousies with which to contend, and there may be choices to make, possibly associated with the family. We must watch ourselves and think at all times of self-protection.

Looking back at Thor's influence on this rune, it is often suggested that this rune signifies the advent of unexpected luck. This could connect with Thursday – Thor's day. Likewise the Thor connection suggests that this rune equates to Thor's hammer, as the symbol resembles this implement. Thor, it is said, used to charge up to his opponent and challenge him. Maybe the rune is calling for you to do likewise! It could however, mean that you need to be on the defensive.

IN REVERSE

Act in haste, repent at leisure is the meaning for this rune if reversed. This is a time to wait, not act. Tensions may run high.

 or  or

Planet Mercury in negative phase   Tarot link – Death
Colour – dark blue   Polarity – male

This rune also relates to the ash tree, the fly agaric toadstool, the wolf and the raven. You will remember that Odin is normally depicted with a raven.

The Anglo-Saxon runic poem reads: 'Os is the source of all language, a pillar of wisdom and a comfort to the wise, a blessing to warriors.'

The Norwegian runic poem reads: 'Oss is source of most travel; but scabbard is of swords.' In this poem *Oss* means 'river mouth'.

The Icelandic runic poem reads: 'Oss is ancient creator and king of Asgard and lord of Valhöll.' In this poem *Oss* means 'God'.

This rune has strong Odin connections and symbolises his protection. For this reason it is sometimes calls 'The God Rune'. It also has strong connections with Yggdrasil, the ash tree in which Odin hung, and with the basket made of ash in which Idun kept the apples which prevented the gods from ageing. In keeping with Odin's knowledge of language, his ability to teach us, and his overall persona, it follows that this rune is also associated with

learning, communication, the spoken word, inspiration, scholarship and those people we hold in high esteem.

This person may be able to help or advise us, or just be there for moral support, and could be seen as a parent or father figure. It can then be said to correspond with the Tarot card The Emperor, but also to cross into The Hierophant, despite its association with the Death card, which stems from Odin's influence.

Odin is shown in many forms, and was, it is said, capable of changing shape at will. A situation may change quickly when this rune is drawn. We should make sure we take note of our dreams when this rune is drawn, because they may contain guidance. We may also find ourselves religiously inspired.

IN REVERSE

Problems with older people are likely. There may also be problems with studies, with the throat or communication, or wasted efforts in other directions. As this rune relates to all forms of communication, be prepared to find your telephone calls not returned, your letters unanswered, your travel plans upset, or your clarity of thought muddied.

*Zodiac sign Gemini   Tarot link – The Hierophant
Colour – red   Polarity – male*

This rune also relates to the mugwort, the goat and the oak tree. Remember that although the zodiac sign is Gemini (the twins) this does not affect the animal connection with the goat (Capricorn), as Vikings had no zodiac connections. The god related to this rune is Ing.

The Anglo-Saxon runic poem reads: 'Rad is easy for the warrior while he is indoors, and very courageous to him who travels the high road upon a stout horse.'

The Norwegian runic poem reads: 'Raid is said to be worst for horses; Regin forged the best sword.' In this poem and the Icelandic, *Raid* means 'Riding'.

The Icelandic runic poem reads: 'Reid is joy of rider and speedy journey and labouring of horse.'

Keywords for this rune include journey, ride and cartwheel. This rune is said to represent journeys both inwardly and outwardly. It suggests that courage may be needed, indicating that the journey may not be easy, but will ultimately prove rewarding. There is also a suggestion that we are looking for a means of transport to take us further in our journey. Obviously this does not just mean an actual form of transport but could relate to an opportunity to move forward. A rune of action and movement, it also concerns anything that goes in twos, and has obvious connections with moving house, transport, legal matters or anything official. You should take care with anything that seems to have two sides to it, especially communications. Remember to think about your own spiritual journey, and whether this is receiving the necessary attention. Also consider the direction your life is taking, and consider changes in lifestyle. Think for yourself – don't discuss matters with others. It is a time when you must be guided by your innermost feelings. This rune is connected to the cycle of seasons and thereby to new experiences and personal transformation. Things are unlikely to remain stationary when this rune is drawn.

IN REVERSE

Things will not go according to plan. You will probably buy something unwisely, or find plans upset. Personal plans may not go well, and you could have unexpected visitors and other such disruptions. Journeys may well have to be aborted, and you could find you lack imagination.

KAUNAZ

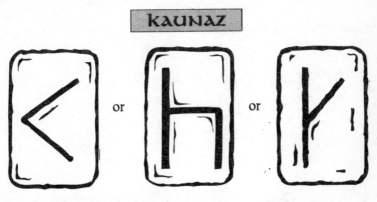

Zodiac sign Aries   *Tarot link – Chariot*   *Colour – flame red*
                      Polarity – female

This rune also relates to the night owl, the cowslip and the pine tree, a branch from this tree often being used as a torch. The god relating to this rune is Heimdall.

The Anglo-Saxon runic poem reads: 'Cen is known to all by its pale bright flame, it always burns where princes sit within.'

The Norwegian runic poem reads: 'Kaun is fatal to children; death makes a corpse pale.' In this poem and the Icelandic, *Kaun* means 'Ulcer'.

The Icelandic runic poem reads: 'Kaun is fatal to children and painful spot and dwelling of putrefaction.'

This is a female rune in all its glory. It concerns female influence, mystery and hope. It also concerns new energy, understanding and positivity. For a woman, drawing this rune signifies the possibility of receiving love from a man, whilst for a man it signifies the joy in giving to a woman. It can also relate to sexuality. The keyword of 'bonfire' for this rune suggests bright flames of passion, and kindling a relationship. There are also suggestions of insight and knowledge, possibly coming from within, as a psychic energy, a light shining in the darkness, an inner light of knowledge. It may be the case that some other knowledge will be superseded or die in order for this new insight to be formed. This can lead to the rune being seen as signifying regeneration from death or life after death.

Fire protected the Vikings from prowling animals, as well as providing warmth and a means of cooking. Likewise this rune can give protection. It can also be taken to mean the formation of something from something else, in the same way as fire is made by rubbing a stick.

Success is indicated by this rune, and protection, guidance and support will be given, especially to those involved in anything artistic. Drawing this rune suggests that you are on the right track and will ultimately be successful.

IN REVERSE

Loss of a friendship or partner could be indicated, as could loss of a possession. There are possibilities of illness or of general ill feeling or unpleasantness. You may feel below par. Sometimes it is necessary for old things to be replaced, or old friendships to fade, in order that new things and new friendships can be made. There may be a lack of direction, and you may feel lost, unable to find a light by which to be guided.

GEBO

Zodiac sign Libra *Tarot link – lovers* *Colour – royal blue*
Polarity – male/female

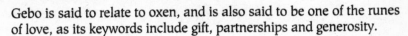

Gebo is said to relate to oxen, and is also said to be one of the runes of love, as its keywords include gift, partnerships and generosity.

Another reason why it is possible that there is a love connection is the very symbol itself, which looks like the crosses we use now to indicate a kiss when writing a letter.

The Anglo-Saxon runic poem reads: 'Gyfu brings credit and honour which support one's dignity, it furnishes help and subsistence to all broken men, devoid of aught else.'

There are no Norwegian or Icelandic runic poems for this symbol.

This rune relates to ash and wych elm trees and to the pansy. It links to the god Gefn, a giver of abundance.

This rune suggests that peace will be our reward, but that you will be called upon to help someone in a serious fashion. This help is vitally needed, and should not be refused, even if it is necessary for some personal sacrifice to take place in the process. This rune suggests that whilst self-sacrifice may be necessary should the favour be called of you, if it is you who need the help, then you may receive help from an unexpected quarter. This rune suggests the need to share, both of yourself and your time.

A good rune to draw if you are working for a charitable cause, this rune could also indicate that extra workloads will be forthcoming, there could be new contracts, etc., but you should not throw yourself totally into this to the exclusion of your own needs.

To those who are unattached, this rune could indicate a possible partnership or new relationship forming. Said by many runemasters to indicate the presence of talent (a gift from the gods), this rune often heralds the joining together of people for the common good.

This rune was dropped from the later Scandinavian Futhark, and has no reversed position.

WUNJO

*Planet Venus in negative phase   Tarot link – Strength
Colour – yellow   Polarity – male*

This rune links with the ash tree, with flax and with the wind. The god connected with this rune is Frigg.

The Anglo-Saxon runic poem reads: 'He enjoys who knows not suffering, sorrow nor anxiety, and has prosperity and happiness and a good enough house.'

Again there are no Norwegian or Icelandic rune poems connected with this symbol.

Wunjo suggests good fortune, marital bliss and domestic happiness and comfort. Harmony will prevail. Drawing this rune suggests, to the single or unattached, that there may be a physical attraction towards someone who will possibly have fair skin or fair hair, whilst to those connected with a business partnership that the union will be successful. Married people are likely to be particularly happy at this time. This is a rune concerned with joy and fellowship, with shared concerns and good news, with harmony and happiness, and with general well-being.

Social events look promising. News may come from afar or from a fair-haired man who is returning from a journey connected with travelling over or near water. Anything connected with creative, artistic or intuitive concerns is well aspected and could bring about an increase in money. Be careful that your projects remain realistic. If they do, you will find yourself fulfilled and happy, and your life

will seem greatly enriched. A good rune to draw when health problems have prevailed.

IN REVERSE

This rune suggests that partners should not be trusted, either in a personal or business sense. Any travel arrangements need to be double-checked and you should be careful over the coming few days, avoiding making any decisions, as bad judgements could result. Any major decisions concerning emotions should be shelved for three months, whilst business decisions need only wait for three days. There is a tendency towards being over-emotional, which could lead to depression or digestive problems. Things will be slow in developing. It is said that this rune in its reversed position is useful in meditation.

This is another rune connected with love, and one of the four 'runes of love'. Said to relate to total love, of mind, body and spirit, this love normally represents the love of a woman, and is said to nullify any more negative runes closeby.

PRACTICE

- Which rune reflects Odin, his persona and powers?

- A friend draws one rune, which is Fehu. She is hoping to get promotion and wishing hard to advance in her chosen career. What does this rune suggest to her?

- The same friend then draws the rune Raido. She would like to work at another division of her company in the north of England which would be nearer to her family. Is this likely?

- Uruz is connected with water buffalo. True or false?

- Jean is a poet. She also draws. She has just submitted some sketches to a magazine with an accompanying poem. A business colleague has suggested that she might be eligible for an arts grant so she can spend more time on her artistic pursuits. She draws the rune Kaunaz. What would this signify?

- Thurisaz links with the planet Mercury. True or false?
- Someone is getting married and draws Wunjo. What does this suggest?

5 hAEGL'S AETT

*W*e will now look at Haegl's aett, which comprises Hagalaz, Nauthiz, Isa, Jena, Eihwaz, Perth, Algiz and Sowelu.

hAGALAZ

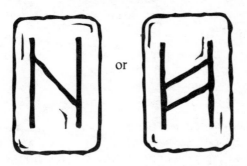

or

Planet Uranus   Tarot link – World   Colour – blue
Polarity – female

This rune does not have direct connections with any particular animal or bird, but is sometimes associated with the hawthorn tree, the ash and the yew, and may also be seen linked with the snake. It also relates to the herb called bryony, to hail, driving sleet and icy conditions, natural forces which can cause damage. It therefore has strong winter connections. The god related to this symbol is Heimdall, the watcher-god, who guards the bridge to the underworld. This rune is said therefore to represent the modern 'Hallowe'en'.

The Anglo-Saxon runic poem reads: 'Hagal is the whitest of grain, it is whirled from the vault of heaven and tossed about by gusts of wind and then melts into water.'

The Norwegian runic poem reads: 'Hagall is the coldest of grains; Christ created the primaeval world.'

The Icelandic runic poem reads: 'Hagall is cold grain and driving sleet and sickness of serpents.'

Disruption, anything unforeseen, delays and elemental forces are all concerned with this rune. There are many things unknown which will come into play when this rune is drawn, and things will be sudden and unexpected. There is nothing you can do to avoid this as it falls outside your influences.

This is a time to grow from experiences and learn a little more about ourselves. Changes are sometimes necessary. You may have to face inconvenience as a result of unforeseen circumstances, which could relate to the weather.

Said to be the rune of the gambler, Hagalaz indicates that things may not turn out as wished, but that it may be wise to take the risk. This rune has strong connections with the number 9 – gamblers please note. Be sure you think about it first though!

It is necessary to remember that things may turn out for the best in the long term, despite the disruption, which could be related to illness. It is worth remembering, however, that this rune, relating to winter as it does, also promises the spring to come, so anything untoward which happens around this time is likely to be short-lived, but will be the foundation upon which future things will grow.

Said to relate to the unconscious mind and to hidden desires, this rune could indicate a pressing need for spiritual guidance, and is therefore another which is often used in meditation.

IN REVERSE

Some runemasters suggest there is no reverse position for this rune. However, should you feel that the symbol can be reversed, the meaning would suggest accidents.

NAUThIZ

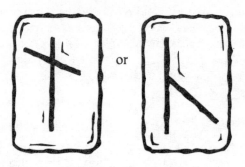

or

Planet Saturn   Tarot link – Devil   Colour – black
Polarity – female

This rune relates to the beech, mountain ash and rowan trees, with the snakeroot, and has a connection with the Argonauts and the god Skuld. Another connection is with the goddess Nott, who was the mother of Dag, whose name is also that of the final rune.

The Anglo-Saxon runic poem reads: 'Nyd is oppressive to the heart, yet often it proves a source of help and salvation to the children of men who heed it betimes.'

The Norwegian runic poem reads: 'Naudr leaves little choice; naked man is chilled by frost.' In both the Norwegian and Icelandic runic poems *Naudr* means 'Need'.

The Icelandic runic poem reads: 'Naud is distress of slave and state of oppression and hard labour.'

Think before acting, as what is presented as a wealth-creating opportunity may be something else. Learn who and what you really are. Your clarity of mind could be affected now, so it might be best to wait before making any firm decisions, especially if they concern money or a job. Emotions could be running high, and relationships may be strained. It is necessary to understand your own limitations and those of others and try to be less demanding and more patient. Limitations are not only restrictions, but also boundaries, and it is important to realise this. Things will change, and it is important that plans are not completely abandoned, but merely held in abeyance.

Be aware of your own needs and requirements (keywords for this rune) and don't do things you would later regret, as it could affect both your own and your family's stability. All this is concerned with work matters. There may be luck associated with older members of the family. This rune is often used by those seeking protection from psychic attack.

IN REVERSE

This suggests that the risk has been taken and the outcome at present is unknown. It is necessary to look to the surrounding runes for the answer here. Also suggested are tensions, frustrations and stress. This is all associated with the chances and opportunities taken, which were possibly some sort of 'get rich quick' scheme, and the lack of clear direction.

ISA

Planet Neptune   ***Tarot link – Hermit***   ***Colour – black***
Polarity – female

This rune relates to reindeer and also to the alder tree and the herb henbane. It is also said to relate to iron, considered a 'holy metal', by the Celts, and some suggest a connection with the wild boar. The god connected to this rune is Verdandi.

The Anglo-Saxon runic poem reads: 'Is is very cold and immeasurably slippery, it glistens clear as glass and is most like to gems. It is a floor wrought by the frost, a fair sight.'

The Norwegian runic poem reads: 'Is we call broad bridge: blind man must be led.'

The Icelandic runic poem reads: 'Iss is bark of rivers and roof of wave and destruction for doomed men.'

This rune relates to ice and icicles. Norse legend says that the universe was formed from fire and ice. Ice is merely solidified water. It will return to water once the thaw sets in; it just takes time. Patience is a virtue which will be needed right now.

There could be emotional cooling in a relationship or business partnership, there may be a separation or parting, and things may have to be shelved for a time. This is only a temporary situation, and could change within seven days, as this rune has a strong connection with that number.

Money expected will not come, and it is best to leave things rather than push for a solution. Things will move in their own time, and it may be necessary to let go of outworn plans. Things will alter in the same way as ice will eventually melt. Thought processes will be slow, and those associated with anything creative are advised to wait and enjoy a rest!

Those around you are unlikely to help. Alternatively, if you consider the clarity of ice, you may find a clear answer to your problem through meditation.

When drawn as one rune in many as part of a casting, the adjacent runes are being reinforced by this holding rune.

IN REVERSE

Again this is another rune which most runemasters suggest has no reversed position, as can be seen by the symbol. I personally feel there is no reversed position, the symbol looking identical whichever way it is placed. However, if you disagree, you could consider the meaning to be physical problems associated with immobility or an ability to move in another direction.

JERA

 o  or

Zodiac sign Virgo   **Tarot link – The Fool**   **Colour – blue**
Polarity – male/female

This rune has no particular connection with any animal or bird, but it does link with the oak tree and with rosemary. Its god is Freyr.

The Anglo-Saxon runic poem reads: 'Jer is a joy to men when the Gods make the earth to bring forth shining fruits for rich and poor alike.'

The Norwegian runic poem reads: 'Ar is a boon to men; I say Frothi was liberal.'

The Icelandic runic poem reads: 'Ar is blessing to men and good summer and fully ripe crops.'

Connected with the harvest, the cycle of the year, cultivation of crops and the reaping of the grain, this rune suggests a time of plenty, of good fortune and the reward of past efforts. Remember, though, that to reap rewards you must have sown seeds in the first place. This is a rune signifying completion. It can also suggest law and order, using a lawyer or professional person, or the natural order of things. Success is likely and hopes run high, and there may be contracts to sign, new projects or a new home. If you are looking for a timescale, the appearance of this rune in a reading indicates that you should look to the next year, the next 12 months, this being the 12th rune and concerned with the cycle of the year. By this, you should be aware that things may take time to reach fruition, or that the period of good luck may only last for a year. This is a good rune

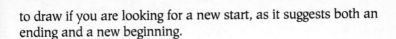

to draw if you are looking for a new start, as it suggests both an ending and a new beginning.

IN REVERSE

This is another rune which looks the same either way up. Most runemasters consider that it has no reverse meanings. Should you disagree, consider it to indicate missed chances.

Zodiac sign Sagittarius   Tarot link – The Hanged Man
Colour – dark blue   Polarity – male

This rune is said to relate to the herb bryony, to the horse and also to the apple tree, although it is sometimes said to relate to the poplar and yew trees or to a bow made from the yew tree (hence the Sagittarian connection). It also relates to the god Ullr, the hunter.

The Anglo-Saxon runic poem reads: 'Eoh is a tree with rough bark, hard and fast in the earth, supported by its roots, a herder of fire and a joy upon an estate.'

There are no Norwegian or Icelandic poems connected to this symbol.

Despite its polarity this rune is most often thought of as feminine, portraying a powerful woman who is capable of bring about good or ill. Changes are indicated which may not be welcome, but will be beneficial all the same. Perhaps it would be best to live for the moment. However, as with its tree, the yew tree, this is a rune of longevity, not only of death, as ancient yew trees often seem to regenerate from daughter trees growing from within them. This is therefore a rune symbolising continuity.

This is a rune of movement (remember the horse connection) and of progress. Business matters and plans need careful and positive thinking, and it is necessary to start looking to the future. Difficulties may not come, despite being expected, and any delays will be temporary. It is necessary to be patient and wait for things to move in the right direction, even if this means you feel uncomfortable for a while. Things will work out well, but it is necessary to be flexible and adapt to new situations. It is also important to be able to let go of outworn or outmoded things and situations.

Considered by many to be a binding rune, this rune is sometimes seen outside the house of students of the runes as it is said to be able to dispel bad storms, both actual or emotional.

IN REVERSE

This is another rune which does not seem to have a reversed position. However, should you disagree, consider the meaning to indicate withdrawal or escapism of some sort.

PERTH

Zodiac sign Scorpio – Tarot link – The Wheel of Fortune
Colour – Black   Polarity – female

This rune is said to relate to woman, to the heron and to the beech, aspen and elm trees, to aconite and the god Frigg, and is often considered to be the rune of mystery, sometimes linking with the flight of the eagle. This rune is said to relate directly to the Ogham character Peith, and as such shares its link with the guelder rose.

The Anglo-Saxon runic poem reads: 'Peoro is a source of recreation and amusement to the great, where warriors sit blithely together in the banquet hall.'

Again there are no Norwegian or Icelandic runic poems for this symbol.

This rune is about warmth, friendship and comforts, probably material. A good time is suggested, with money coming from unexpected quarters. Things may be hidden or unexpected, as this rune is connected with anything secret, yet celebrations will be many, and social events are numerous.

This rune is sometimes seen as a rune of fate. It is also sometimes associated with game-playing, leading to the suggestion that you will only be as good as the game you play. You may meet up with friends from the past, and there is an emphasis on memories, and an increased capacity for problem-solving. There is also a link with esoteric or hidden knowledge, and it is possible that drawing this rune will indicate a greater interest in such things. It is also possible that there will be an increase in dreams which could prove prophetic.

This rune suggests a seeking of knowledge and of inner transformation. Things may never be quite the same again. It is said that should this be the first rune drawn in a reading, the reading should be put aside for a while. As with anything hidden or secret, things may not always be what they seem to be, and it is necessary for you to look past the surface and into the depths to see a situation for what it really is.

IN REVERSE

This suggests disappointments, because too much has been expected. Favours done for others will be either not appreciated or not returned, and things will be going on behind your back which could cause unnecessary worry.

ALGIZ

***Zodiac sign Pisces   Tarot link – The Moon   Colour – gold
Polarity – male/female***

This rune is said to relate to an elk, sedge, eelgrass, reed or rush and to lime and yew trees. The god connected to this rune is Heimdall.

The Anglo-Saxon runic poem reads 'Secg (or eolh) is mostly to be found in a marsh, it grows in water and makes a ghastly wound. The blood burns of every man who makes a grasp at it.'

This is another case of there being no Norwegian or Icelandic runic poems for this symbol.

In its upright position this is a rune of protection or healing, and as such it is often used in meditational healing. Said to be able to protect an individual's whole family, as well as friends, against hostile influences, this rune signifies that a sacrifice may be necessary and that other people may try to push you into doing something against your will. Career matters are well favoured, especially anything concerning artistic matters, and help will be given to you by a friend. New interests will be apparent, possibly artistic ones. It is important that you take charge of your emotions and make time for yourself. It is also important to hold on to what you have.

Another good rune for meditational purposes because of its

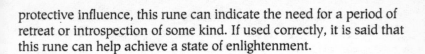

protective influence, this rune can indicate the need for a period of retreat or introspection of some kind. If used correctly, it is said that this rune can help achieve a state of enlightenment.

IN REVERSE

This suggests health concerns, and that you should not overburden yourself with the problems of others, and don't let other people use you. Be careful not to act in haste. Don't get involved with people who may be doing things which you consider immoral or incorrect. Creative interests may seem blocked at this time when the rune is in reverse.

SOWELU

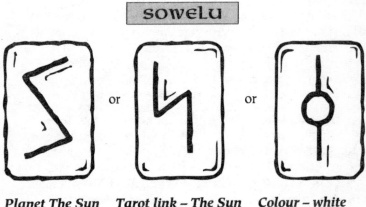

Planet The Sun   *Tarot link – The Sun*   *Colour – white*
Polarity – male

This rune relates strongly to the sun, and also to the eagle, the juniper, bay and oak trees. It also relates to mistletoe and the god Balder. It concerns the life force, and is another rune of love.

The Anglo-Saxon runic poem reads: 'Sigel is a joy to seafarers, when they journey over the fishes' bath until the courser of the deep bears them to land.'

The Norwegian runic poem reads: 'Sol is the light of the world; I bow before the divine judgment.'

The Icelandic runic poem reads: 'Sol is shield of sky and shining ray and destroyer of ice.'

This rune is said to represent the love of a man for a woman, and rules mental and physical health. Love is all-important in the world; it is through love that we all grow and become truly whole. If this rune is present, it casts sunshine on the reading, and whilst not reversing any untoward meanings concerning other runes, it at least sheds a little more hope on the situation, even if it does appear to be far off. It is a rune of clear vision. There is an obvious link here with the Tarot card The Sun, as stated above. Good health, good luck, a happy romance and wholeness are all suggested by this rune. This rune helps to give strength, as the sun seems to give us added vitality. It is a rune of winning and victory, and it is another good rune for healing.

It is important to distance yourself from any connection with the Nazi regime when drawing this rune, and explain to others who may have realised that the symbol was used by the SS that it has only favourable meanings when in its upright position. It means achievement, victory and success and perhaps this was one of the reasons it was chosen by the Germans at that time in their history.

It is possible that this rune suggests contact with your inner life force or spirit, and again this is another rune which indicates a growing spirituality, a period of learning or anything involving vocational training. Light may well be entering your life, and it is important to recognise the need to balance your spirituality with your material needs. A time of decision is also indicated, and it may be necessary to decide in which direction your life is to lead.

Another rune of protection, this rune concerns energy, and harnessing of the energy for useful purpose. Try not to overtire yourself, and save your energies and learn to relax a little. Sporting interests are well favoured with this rune, and it is a useful rune to draw if you are embarking upon a sporting contest, or indeed if you are about to go on holiday.

IN REVERSE

To most runemasters, this rune has no reversed meaning. If you disagree, you may take it to mean that relaxation should be of paramount importance, and it is important not to overstrain tired

muscles. You must recharge batteries and not allow people to make unnecessary demands on your time.

We have now covered 16 runes in detail. We have another eight runes still to discuss, plus the all-important blank rune or wyrd.

Before we leave this chapter behind, however, we must test ourselves to see that we have understood and digested the information given. Again, no answers will be given. Good luck!

PRACTICE

- Is or Isa means Ice. What does this rune suggest if drawn?
- Which runes are suggested as useful in meditation?
- Which rune begins Haegl's aett?
- What rune is sometimes associated with gamblers?
- What period of time is suggested by Jera?

6

TYR'S AETT

We are now moving into Tyr's aett. Tyr, also seen as Teiwaz, Tir or Tiw is a god of war, and is the final aett before the all-important blank rune or wyrd, which concerns fate or karma, and falls outside any of the aetts. It comprises Teiwaz, Berkana, Ehwaz, Mannaz, Laguz, Inguz, Othila and Dagaz.

TEIWAZ

or

Planet Mars   Tarot link – Justice   Colour – flame red
Polarity – male

This rune relates to the god Tir or Tyr, as already discussed, and has links with the hazel and oak trees, purple sage, and a guiding planet or star, following on from the Anglo-Saxon runic poem.

The Anglo-Saxon runic poem reads: 'Tiw is a guiding star, well does it keep faith with princes: it is ever on its course over the mists of night and never fails.'

The Norwegian runic poem reads: 'Tyr is one-handed among the gods; oft has the smith to blow.'

The Icelandic runic poem reads: 'Tyr is one-handed among the gods and leavings of wolf and king of temples.'

The god Tyr, it is worth remembering, was a fighting god, a spiritual warrior, similar to the Roman god Mars. He was courageous and lost his right hand having sworn a false oath, hence the mention of one-handed in the Norwegian and Icelandic runic poems.

Another rune said to be a 'rune of love' despite its male connections with battles and warfare, this rune may represent selfishness within a relationship. If the arrow of the symbol is pointing downwards, this suggests a superficial relationship (connected with the Page of Swords in the Tarot deck perhaps), a woman should not trust her man, and for a man, the relationship is short-lived, probably because he is too demanding. If it is pointing upwards, it represents guidance from above, problems in love being overcome and things turning out well.

This rune suggests that if the questioner is a man, the love will be his love for a woman, whilst if the questioner is a woman, someone strong and handsome will love her. Passions will run high either way, but jealousies may also creep in.

Remember, whether you be man or woman, that according to legend Tyr lost his hand through swearing a false oath, so things said may not be true. Yet again, it is said that he was trying to bind the Fenris-wolf, and so an element of self-sacrifice may also be called for.

It is useful to meditate on this rune in its upright position if you seek answers to a problem. Success in business is very likely when this rune is drawn in its upright position. Any opportunities should be seized as they may be successful. It is important, however, to be aware of your own strengths and those of others. Legal matters are well favoured, as are sporting concerns. This rune suggests going towards a project with strength of purpose and clear aims, allowing nobody and nothing to get in your path. Like the symbol, the arrow, we must be sure in which direction we are going.

A very masculine rune in the main, this rune also concerns physical attraction, and is said to have connections with the day Tuesday (Tyr's day). Its masculine nature leads to further associations with justice and leadership and dealing with those in authority. It further suggests strength, honour and invincibility.

IN REVERSE

We have already discussed the love connection. It can also, however, mean problems with property, health or obsessive behaviour.

BERKANA

Zodiac sign Cancer   Tarot link – The Empress   Colour – green   Polarity – female

This rune relates to the birch and fir trees, the herb lady's mantle, to the bear and the swan. It is a rune of fertility and of homelife, quite fitting for the sign of Cancer. It is also connected with the god Nerthus.

The Anglo-Saxon runic poem reads: 'Beorc bears no fruit, yet without seed it brings forth shoots, for it is generated from its leaves. Splendid are its branches and gloriously adorned, its lofty crown reaching the skies.'

The Norwegian runic poem reads: 'Bjarkan is greenest-leafed of branches; Loki was lucky in his deception.'

The Icelandic runic poem reads: 'Bjarkan is leafy branch and little tree and youthful shrub.'

Students of astrology will know Cancer's connection with the Moon and with spirituality, and students of the Tarot will also be aware of the Moon's connection with intuitive matters. It is therefore no surprise to learn that this rune suggests the need to look at your spirituality and be a little less materialistic.

It is often necessary to look within ourselves and at our aims and desires, to cleanse and clean those parts with which we are less than happy and to examine our motives. New projects are indicated, which could concern spiritual or material matters, but now is a time for personal growth, as well as for looking after family concerns.

This is definitely a time for new beginnings, and can be linked to new babies, new jobs, new family members, weddings, etc. There will be much cause for celebration, both within the family and outside it.

Remember that anything new needs nurturing to allow it to reach its fullest potential.

This is a rune of regeneration, connected with the primary Ogham character Beth, which also symbolises regenerative powers and new beginnings.

IN REVERSE

This rune suggests problems in growth, possibly through incorrect choices. It may be necessary to stop and start again.

News which concerns the family may be worrying. This could concern health matters. Parties and celebrations may be cancelled, and there could be a feeling of dis-ease, as opposed to illness or ill health.

ehwaz

***Planet Mercury in its positive aspect   Tarot link –
The Lovers   Colour – white   Polarity – male/female***

This rune is said to relate strongly to the horse (hence the poem below) as well as to the apple, oak and ash trees. It also relates to the ragwort and to the god Freyja.

The Anglo-Saxon runic poem reads: 'Eh is a joy to princes in the presence of warriors, a steed in the pride of its hooves, when rich men discuss it, it is ever a comfort to the restless.'

This is another case of there being no Norwegian or Icelandic runic poems for this symbol.

This rune concerns one's own status and that of others, and is said to reinforce the meanings of adjacent runes. Said by some to be a rune of scientific interests, the drawing of this rune would suggest a new project, probably science-related or involving higher education. Changes are likely on a large scale when this rune is drawn. Emotions will again be running strong, and should be watched. Its link to the horse also suggests travel, probably a new home and a strong partnership. Things are changing for the better. However, take care with your transport, more so if the rune is reversed. Some people would say that a horse is only as good as its rider, but qualify this by saying that there must be an element of loyalty, trust and respect for a successful team. This should be remembered in any kind of partnership.

A strong connection with Mercury, the planet of communication suggests that those interested in embarking upon a spiritual journey should meditate upon this rune, as it is the seer's rune. Harmony and control are vital if the journey is to be successful. Maybe we just need the push to get underway!

IN REVERSE

There are likely to be transport problems and animals may fall ill. Sea journeys and delays are indicated.

MANNAZ

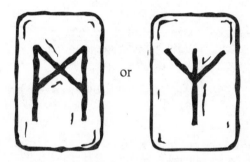

Zodiac sign Aquarius   Tarot link – The Magician
Colour – red   Polarity – male/female

This rune is said to relate to mankind, and man as a species, as well as to the hawk. Because Nordic tradition suggests that man was made from trees, it is suggested that this rune relates to the ash tree for man and to the elm tree for woman, whilst other authorities have suggested the alder, maple, holly bush and madder herb, the latter being used in the colouring of the runes. Three gods are connected with this rune: Odin, Frigg and Heimdall.

The Anglo-Saxon runic poem reads: 'Mann is a dear one to his kinsmen, yet each must fail his fellow, as the body is committed to the earth.'

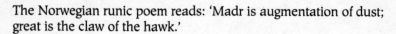

The Norwegian runic poem reads: 'Madr is augmentation of dust; great is the claw of the hawk.'

The Icelandic runic poem reads: 'Madr is the joy of man and augmentation of dust and adorner of ships.'

This rune relates to the questioner or enquirer, to the individual, and to correct behaviour. It is a rune of relationships and of shared experiences. It concerns how other people see you and how you see yourself, and it reminds us all of our mortality. Remember to look as carefully at yourself as you do at other people. Look at the way you act, both when you are with others and when you are alone. Just as you may not be who or what you think you are, other people may not be what you think they are.

You should consider consulting someone in a professional capacity before entering into anything binding. Don't act in haste. Try to be different if you can, but don't plan too far ahead. Learn to look within a little more. Watch other people and their motives.

Think and remember past events which may have a bearing on the situations presently to hand. Watch your health, too, when you draw this rune.

There are likely to be conflicts which will add to stress levels, and legal problems are indicated.

Anything concerning the New Age is likely to be interesting to you, as are matters concerning the environment and the welfare of others. This rune simply means 'help'.

IN REVERSE

This suggests potential enemies who may not be of your own culture, or problems with authority.

Look to the following rune for help as to who this is or in what way problems can be avoided. It may be prudent to start looking within yourself for some answers.

Some runemasters suggest that this rune in reverse shows the questioner's father, who may be overstrict.

LAGUZ

Planet Moon   Tarot link – The Star   Colour – green
Polarity – female

This rune relates strongly to water, in keeping with the pull of the moon on the tides. It also relates to the seal, gull and osier or willow tree. It also has connections with the leek and with the god Njord. Its connection with the sea and with water leads to further associations with seashells and waterfalls.

The Anglo-Saxon runic poem reads: 'Lagu seems interminable to men if they venture on the rolling bark and the waves of the sea afright them and the courses of the deep heed not its bridle.'

The Norwegian runic poem reads: 'Logr is where cascade falls down mountain-side; but ornaments are made of gold.'

The Icelandic runic poem reads: 'Logr is welling stream and broad geyser and land of fish.'

This rune concerns success and material concerns, which may be either acquired or lost, as the power is likely to lie with others. Things will ebb and flow, as with the tide. Sometimes the sea can be kind, and at other times, as in storms, it seems harsh. Water may be fluid, but it is also strong. The connection with water must be remembered at all times, as without water the human being cannot exist. There will be nothing to be done, as you have no control over circumstances, especially when they involve other people. Success will come in its own time.

This rune also concerns travel, which is likely to be long-distance, especially overseas, and could concern business or personal matters. Imagination is heightened when this rune is drawn, and is likely to reinforce any interest in psychic or spiritual matters. You possibly need to undergo some spiritual cleansing. Use your intuition and be prepared to doubt yourself at the start. As with any journey, the prospect can sometimes be daunting. This rune also relates strongly to feminine fertility, and it can represent a pregnancy or children. This is a very strong rune.

IN REVERSE

This rune suggests you may be trying too hard and being too pushy. You need to keep within your limits, and that includes consumption of foodstuffs as well as alcohol. Watch your emotions and guard against being too emotional or dependent on other people or on outside agencies. Try to use your logic.

INGUZ

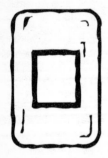

This is also sometimes seen as

Planet Venus in its positive phase. Some runemasters suggest that it also has links with the Moon.
Tarot link – Judgement   Colour – yellow
Polarity – male/female

This rune connects with Ing, the Danish god of fertility, the hero-god, and as such with male fertility, the boar and the cuckoo. The connection with the boar possibly stems from the feast to the god Freyr, when the head of the sacred boar was served crowned with laurel and rosemary. This rune is said to be a doorway to the astral, and connects with the apple tree and the herb self-heal.

The Anglo-Saxon runic poem reads: 'Ing was amongst the East-Danes first seen by men, till later east he went over the wave; his wain followed after; the Headings named the hero so.'

This is another symbol which does not have a Norwegian or Icelandic runic poem attached to it.

Strongly connected with male health and fertility, this rune suggests new birth, contact with close relatives and creative energy.

Often drawing this rune shows the likelihood of a move or new job, or the potential for change. This is the end of a phase, and things will either be solved or take on a new direction. This rune heralds the period before a new project is started, and the energy to start. It is the seed or bulb which has been planted to grow and flourish in the future. It would be stupid to expect to plant the bulb and see the flowers the next day. These things take time.

It is sometimes necessary to have a good clear-out, both actual and mental, and this is suggested when this rune appears. This could mean the ending of a relationship which is going nowhere or just getting yourself more motivated and embarking upon a new project or interest.

Holidays are well favoured and rest and relaxation are important.

IN REVERSE

Most runemasters, myself included, have no reverse meaning for this rune. However, if you disagree, consider that it means restrictions and tensions, lack of progress and frustrations.

OThILA

Zodiac sign Capricorn   Tarot link – Moon
Colour – Yellow ochre   Polarity – Male

This rune is said to relate to the hawthorn tree, to clover and to Odin.

The Anglo-Saxon runic poem reads: 'Epel is dear to all men, if they may enjoy there at home whatever is right and proper in constant prosperity.'

There are no Norwegian or Icelandic runic poems for this symbol.

Concerned with matters of the home, land or property, this rune suggests that a marriage or engagement is likely. It relates to belonging, to heritage and to togetherness. It also suggests something which is permanent and immovable.

Anything involving children is well aspected, and money is likely to come via an inheritance or win.

It is necessary to examine your own spirituality, as your body is also home to your spirit, and should not be neglected. You should never forget your own spiritual heritage.

New experiences are likely, but it is necessary to make a determined effort and not sit back and wait for things to land in your lap without some work!

You are likely to come across opposition from the establishment or those with traditional views. Likewise, you may be asked to sign documents relating to wills or property.

Older people, especially, will figure strongly at this time. However, they will most likely be well disposed towards you and seek to help if possible.

Moves are not unlikely, and you may be asked to perform some duties. It is important to remember that your home is more than somewhere you go to at the end of the day – it is a special place where you can go to repair your wounds, both physical and mental, and where you can be with your family and friends in peace and safety. If you think of your home this way, and remember to think of your body as a similar home to your spirit, you will realise the importance of addressing the spiritual part of yourself regularly.

IN REVERSE

This suggests accidents or damage from or to mechanical devices. Theft or loss is also suggested, and you may have problems around the house. Take care of your health. Disputes over inheritances are likely.

DAGAZ

 Also sometimes seen as

Zodiac sign Leo   Tarot link – Temperance
Colour – blue   Polarity – male

This rune is said to relate to the rowan and Norway spruce trees, and simply means 'day'. It is also connected to sage and the god Heimdall.

The Anglo-Saxon runic poem reads: 'Daeg the glorious light of the sun is sent by the High One, is beloved of men, a source of hope and happiness to prosperous and poor alike, of service to all.'

This symbol is another which does not have a Norwegian or Icelandic runic poem attached to it.

Daylight, new starts and enlightenment are all part of the meaning of this rune. This is the rune of midday and also midsummer. If you are waiting for a breakthrough from a period of stalemate, this is the rune for you. You are metaphorically coming from a period of darkness into the light of day, at which time things take on a different perspective, and may need re-evaluating.

Ideals are likely to be high when this rune is drawn and ambition strong. There are opportunities to be seized and wishes to fulfil.

You are likely to be concerned with your own and your family's security, and now is the time to plan for the future and embark upon new projects. Anything different may appeal, and you could consider changing your lifestyle, moving to a totally different area or country, or putting in for promotion.

Chances to increase your income are likely and things are likely to start to change slowly for the better.

Children or youngsters will feature prominently at this time. Things are likely to alter beyond recognition and you could well have startling changes of attitude and a new understanding of life and the things within it which are important to you.

This is a good rune to draw, but often indicates the need for hard work. As the saying goes, 'If it's worth having, it's worth working for!' Good health and prosperity are likely. This rune is linked with the Ogham character Duir and the Hebrew letter Daleth.

IN REVERSE

Again, this is another rune which I feel cannot be reversed. However, you may choose to disagree, in which case it may mean the end of a period rather than the actual start of a new one.

Ϧealing, protection and finance

We have now covered all the runes, but before continuing, we must look back to the runes which can be linked together for help in healing, protection and finance as discussed earlier.

For emotional healing, consider ᚱᛋᚠᛗᛞᚢᛉ whilst for physical healing consider ᚷᛏᛋᚠ·ᛁᚲᛢ . In cases where protection is needed, the most common linkage is ᚲᛒᛟᚦᛟᚹ . Financial help may be obtained by using ᚠᛜᚷᛃᚱᛟ .

The Anglo-Saxon rune poems

Those specifically interested in the Anglo-Saxon runes may like to know that there are a further five runes, namely Ac, Aesc, Yr, Iar and Ear. Ac relates to the oak tree, Aesc to the ash, Yr to the bow, Iar to the otter and Ear to the grave. These five runes do not form part of the Elder Futhark which is the main focus of this book, but all have Anglo-Saxon runic verses ascribed to them. Their symbols are

ᚪ for Ac, ᚫ for Aesc, ᚣ for Yr, ᛡ for Iar and

ᛠ for Ear.

The Anglo-Saxon runic verses for these read as follows:

'Ac for the children of men on earth is flesh-fodder; it rares oft over the gannet's bath; the ocean tests whether the oak keeps noble faith.'

'Aesc is extremely high, dear to men, strong on its base, sturdy of trunk, even though many men fight against it.'

'Yr is to every aethling and eorl delight and dignity, is fair on a steed, trusty in company, a part of war-gear.'

'Iar is a river fish, and yet it has pleasure of food on land; it has a fair home, surrounded by water, where it dwells in delight.'

'Ear is grim to every eorl when the flesh inflexibly begins to chill, the corpse choose earth for consort pale; pleasures pall, joys vanish; bonds are betrayed.'

The Norwegian and Icelandic runic poems have as their final symbol the symbol ⟨ or ⟩ for Yr. Again this does not appear in the Elder Futhark, and so the runic poems for this symbol are given here.

The Norwegian runic poem reads: 'Yr (yew) is greenest of trees in winter, when it burns, it splutters.'

The Icelandic runic poem reads: 'Yr (yew) is bent bow, and brittle iron and Farbauti of arrow.'

We need to have our quiz before finishing this chapter, and again the answers are not given.

PRACTICE

- Which runes suggest birth, new starts or new beginnings?

- Which rune has associations with the zodiac sign of Capricorn?

- Which rune has associations with the moon?

- If you are looking for a change of job or promotion, or indeed more money, which rune(s) would you consider favourable?

- Tyr's set is the second of the aetts. True or false?

- What two symbols indicate the rune Dagaz?

- Berkana is connected with the element of air. True or false?

THE BLANK RUNE AND FURTHER USE

We have now covered all the symbols on the runes, and have looked in detail at their meanings. It is now necessary to consider the rune which has no symbol, but which has a strong meaning, and that rune is the blank rune or wyrd. We will then progress to learn which runes to use to create new names, and which runes should go before and after the name to symbolise the aspirations of the holder. We shall also take a look at the runic Kabbala, before discussing ways of casting the runes.

WYRD

This rune has no connections with any planet, zodiac sign, bird, plant or animal. It is the rune of karma or fate, and concerns things which cannot be predestined, but which also cannot be avoided. As it has no symbol, it has no place within the runic alphabetical system, and is only used when casting the runes.

The word *wyrd* is actually Anglo-Saxon, not Nordic, and relates to the Viking word *Orlog*, meaning destiny, doom or fate. This rune is another with a strong 'Odin connection'. The Vikings looked to Odin as their primary god, the one to whom they entrusted their lives, yet who often showed a path which instilled fear and trepidation.

For those unfamiliar with the word *karma*, this Indian word basically means destiny. I strongly believe that we are all subject to destiny or fate. When we start in this life, we are given a book on which the outline of the story is written. It is up to us to fill in the missing pages, so we retain free will and choice. The outline of the story is what is meant by destiny or karma. Often this concept is linked to past lives, and what should or should not have been done. It is also linked to the way we have behaved in these past lives, and putting right the wrongs we have done in order to progress and to learn.

Some people will call karma the law of cause and effect. This, however, can lead to the incorrect assumption that karma is punishment for past misdemeanours. Karma is more realistically the opportunity to make amends for things we may have done wrong before, either within this lifetime or in a previous one. Not everything can be controlled by us. There are some things which happen and leave us with no choice one way or the other. Such things are said to be ruled by fate, all of which is indicated by this rune. That doesn't mean to say we forget about our ability to make choices, as this is still an important part of the meaning of this rune.

It is said that the only way to break the karmic chain is by the Law of Grace, which basically means learning forgiveness. Every action creates karma, but by using karmic progression you can ease matters and learn. Karma can be explained as the inability to live up to something you know you should do or could have done. Drawing this rune suggests to some degree that we must place our trust in those things which we may not understand totally, whilst admitting our fears, but not remaining fearful. Karma will determine your destiny only if you let it, and remember you only get out of a situation what you put into it. There is only an opportunity to better oneself. Bad karma can only be created by ignorance, lack of wisdom, and lack of love, as well as by fear and negativity.

The Wyrd rune in a casting

When this rune is drawn, the indications are that there is to be a major change, or that a stage has been reached in the questioner's life which is likely to prove a turning point. Sometimes this rune can suggest a death. This is by no means a certainty, and it would not be

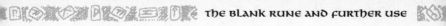

advisable merely to give this interpretation when casting the runes. It may mean the death of a situation, in much the same way as the Death card in the Tarot. Sometimes it is necessary for a situation to end for a new one to begin. We must have faith that what comes will ultimately be for the good, or at the very least be an opportunity to learn. Maybe we should look to the death of self-image or another part of our personality when this rune is drawn. Things will definitely change, and we must consider changing with them if we are to survive intact. Powerful forces are at large, and we must be subject to them.

To the Vikings, the blank rune was more than ever Odin's rune, as he was the god who dictated man's fate. Should you be seeking an answer to one specific question and decide to draw one rune alone, the blank rune suggests that now is not the time to ask the question and you should try again at another date.

Want to change your name?

Before considering ways of laying the runes for help, we will take a look at the runes to use if you are considering changing your name, or luck, or merely using the runes in a necklace or amulet.

Listed below are the runes which correspond to our alphabet. Please note that they do not tally with the alphabetical link discussed previously, and should only be used in connection with name changes.

Those who understand the principles of numerology and how different vibrations can change our direction in life will be quite at home with the idea that changing names can either help or hinder our future progress.

Let's pretend we are looking for a name for a writer. We decide upon the name Brenda Shaw. Using the table given above we come up with the appropriate symbols. However, before leaving it at that, we must look at the runes to go before and after the name, to enclose it in a protective element. The runes which go before the name are called the 'leaders' and those that go after the name chosen the 'sealers'. The table below shows which runes to use for specific purposes. They must not change, and should be followed exactly for the best effect.

	THE LEADER	THE SEALER
MUSIC	ᚠ	ᚷ
THE ARTS	ᚷ	ᛟ
MYSTICISM	ᛞ	ᛇ
MAGIC	ᚹ	ᛃ
TRAVEL	ᚱ	ᚲ
HOME	ᛉ	ᛒ
STUDY	ᚨ	ᛞ
LAW	ᛋ	ᚦ
MEDICINE /HEALTH	ᛉ	ᛗ

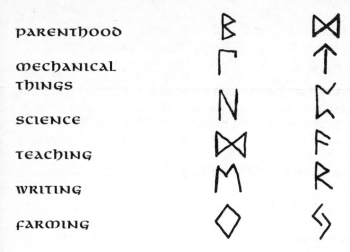

PARENTHOOD	ᛒ	ᛡ
MECHANICAL THINGS	ᛚ	↑
SCIENCE	ᚾ	ᛦ
TEACHING	ᛝ	ᚠ
WRITING	ᛗ	ᚱ
FARMING	◇	ᛋ

If we were using the name Brenda Shaw, this would fall into the writing category as already discussed and have as its leader rune ᛗ and its sealer rune ᚱ . The finished runeword, or more properly 'sigil' would therefore be ᛗ ᛒ ᚱ ᛗ ᛏ ᛝ ᚠ ᛋ ᚾ ᚨ ᛈ ᚱ.

Give it a try and see if it works for you.

RUNIC KABBALA

There is a huge interest in anything relating to the Kabbala, a word which is said to mean 'hidden' or 'secret' and it is interesting to note that there are several connections between the Kabbala and the runes. The first is that both names mean 'secret' or 'hidden'. Another link lies within the concept of the Kabbalistic Tree of Life, as there is also a tree in the tale of the runes which is called Yggdrasil, as we know. This tree was also known as the world ash tree, and tradition suggests that it contained within it the Nine Worlds (the whole of creation), another way of saying the Tree of Life perhaps. Yet another link lies with the fact that it is said that both the Kabbala and the original runic meanings were not written down and were handed down orally to students.

Those with a knowledge of the Kabbala will know that the Tree of Life contains 22 paths. These paths run from their appropriate ten sephiroth (stations). These sephiroth concern various things, and are shown in Figure 7.1. However, it is important to realise what each means, as you can use these paths in what are known as pathworkings upon which to meditate, linking in with the runic symbols to create a strong meditation.

Understanding the Kabbala

To those who understand little about the Kabbala, a word or two of explanation here.

The Kabbala concerns the creation of the world. It is said that God created the world by means of 32 secret paths of wisdom, which are 10 sephiroth and the 22 letters of the Hebrew alphabet. Each sephiroth is a level of knowledge to be attained, the lower seven corresponding to the chakra centres in the body. The sephiroth are said to comprise the personal name of God (Yahweh).

It is possible to attain a spiritual awakening by meditating on the Kabbalistic Tree of Life in similar ways to those used by students of yoga. Using the pathways discussed here, with the linking of the runes, it is possible to increase this awareness and raise consciousness. The sephiroth should be the initial focus at the beginning, but then one should draw from the experiences gained.

Some Kabbalists use sound or colour when meditating on the sephiroth, whilst others link them to numbers, angels, metals, planets and chakra centres. Experience will show the best way for you. However, it is important to understand the sephiroth. Their basic meanings are given below.

1. Kether – crown
2. Chokmah – wisdom
3. Binah – understanding
4. Chesed – mercy

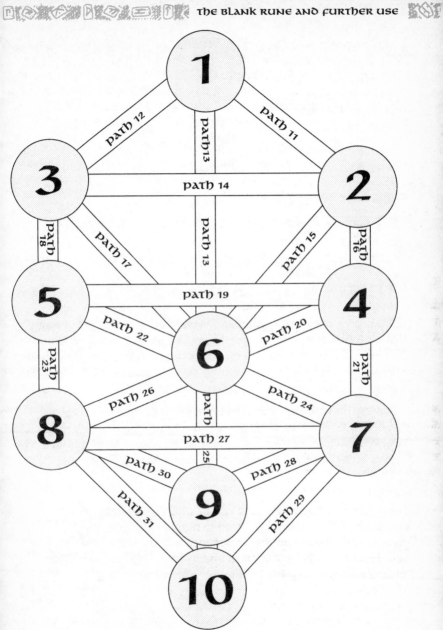

Figure 7.1   *The Kabbalistic Tree of Life*

5. Geburah – severity
6. Tiphareth – beauty
7. Netzach – victory
8. Hod – glory
9. Yesod – foundation
10. Malkuth – kingdom

We have 24 runes, which means they will fit within this plan. Paths 11 and 12 are assigned two runes each, one ascending and the other descending, thus using up the 24 runes available (ignoring the blank rune this time).

The diagram shown on page 83 contains all the 22 paths, clearly marked.

BIND RUNES

Bind runes are runic combinations, where two runes are seemingly fused together to form a symbol. These symbols, more correctly called bind runes, were often used on amulets and jewellery to help the wearer with certain things. It is not unusual to use runes in this way.

Coming up with your own bind runes can be an interesting experience, but Figure 7.2 gives you a few to give you some ideas. All you have to remember is to use runes with linking meanings. In good luck (below), for example, we use 'gift' and 'luck'.

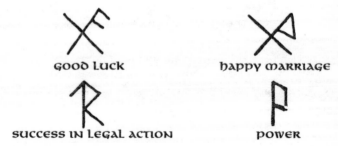

GOOD LUCK

HAPPY MARRIAGE

SUCCESS IN LEGAL ACTION

POWER

Figure 7.2   *Some bind runes*

PROBLEMS WITH CONCEPTION

MENTAL POWER

LOVE (MAN FOR WOMAN)

LOVE (WOMAN FOR MAN)

Those interested in runic symbols may well like to receive amulets with these bind runes upon them. They make very unusual and potent presents.

Ways of casting the runes

There are probably hundreds of different ways to lay the runes for a casting. What is given here is only a selection. It is by no means exhaustive.

I would suggest that you try some of these, going for the ones with which you feel comfortable before trying your own ideas out. The reasons for this are many, not least of which it is important to familiarise yourself with the runes and how they are read as a group before progressing.

It should also be remembered that you may have some personal thoughts on the meanings of the runes at the time you are carrying out the casting, which you should not dismiss out of hand. The meanings given in this book are basic, and again by no means exhaustive. You may for example wish to use all the reverse meanings given, even though some runes look the same either way up. Experience is the best teacher, and you must always do what

you feel comfortable doing. Don't go along with something just because others do – make up your own mind.

As we said earlier in the book, many runemasters draw three sets of three runes to indicate past, present and future. These are cast and laid from right to left as shown below:

Another means of casting the runes consists of five runes, called Odin's casting. Again these are laid down from right to left, with the third rune slightly raised from the remainder. I read these as being two pages within a book with the third rune being that which is either holding the pages together, or conversely, stopping them from being turned. I use a similar layout in Tarot readings.

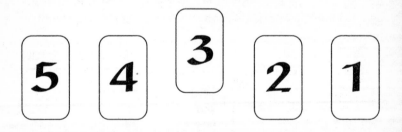

Similar layout could be used with seven runes.

You could also consider using a 12 rune casting, linking each rune either with a month or with a sign of the zodiac. This is usually laid out in a circle, as in Figure 7.3, although I have seen many variations of this.

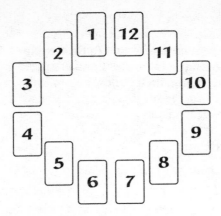

Figure 7.3   *A 12 rune casting*

A very popular means of casting the runes is the Runic Cross (Figure 7.4). This is laid out as shown below, and using this layout can prove very rewarding.

Figure 7.4   *The Runic Cross*

Yet another suggestion would be what is sometimes called the rune-cast method. Those who have read my *Gems and Crystals for Beginners* may see some similarities in the way this is done with one of the ways of reading crystals discussed in that book. Basically, you 'shuffle' the runes within their pouch, and having formed a circle of string on the floor, empty the pouch into it. Those runes nearest to you have the greatest meaning. Should any have fallen outside the string circle, these can be ignored; likewise if they fall on the string or have fallen face downwards.

There are many more ways of casting the runes, and no doubt you will find one suitable for you. Experiment and practise.

Before we leave this chapter behind and do some practice, let's not forget our little quiz! Again, no answers given.

pRACTICE

- What does the word 'wyrd' mean?
- What links can you find between the Kabbala and the runes?
- Which way of casting the runes has a link with Odin?
- Why should you have, at either end of a sigil, two runes which may not have a bearing on the word created?
- The blank rune fits into Freyr's aett. True or false?
- When casting runes, you lay them from right to left. True or false?

This is the chapter in which we do some practice in casting the runes. Some of the answers will be given, and some won't. Remember, there is no set way of helping either yourself or someone else when casting the runes. A lot of it is open to individual interpretation and experience. It also depends to some degree on what the questioner is seeking help with, and what he or she wants to know.

START PRACTISING!

Let's pretend we are doing a casting for a friend at work. She is middle-aged and has two sons who have left home and have their own families. She feels stuck in a rut. She thinks she is capable of doing more than she does, yet her age always seems to go against her when she applies for promotion. She wonders if she should take up an offer of work elsewhere in a totally different field to that in which she has worked for the last 25 years. You explain to her that there are various ways of casting the runes, and she opts to use the five-rune casting discussed in the last chapter.

The runes she draws from the pouch are as follows, and in this order:

Perth, Teiwaz, Nauthiz, Jera and Fehu.

Remember, these, unlike the list given above, are laid from right to left. Let's also pretend, for ease, that all the runes are the right way up.

How would you choose to explain the meanings behind these, taking into account the circumstances of the lady concerned, and what she wants to know?

Remember the keywords to each rune. Remember also that they should be looked at both in isolation and together. Remember that Nauthiz, being the third rune, may be the binding or the thing stopping movement. How does this relate to the actual meaning of the Nauthiz rune? Is this fitting with a feeling of constraint? Should she give up her dreams and plans? Look at the next two runes and form a conclusion.

Initially, you may want to write the runes down, work out the meanings and put the answers together in written form. If you are more adventurous, perhaps you can explain the meanings without doing this.

So we have now covered the casting for this lady, and she still isn't totally sure what she should do. She decides to opt for one rune, with a question requiring either a 'yes' or a 'no' answer. She asks the question, 'Should I stay in the job I'm in now?' Remember, she can't add on the end of this question 'or should I change jobs' because that would mean the answer needed more than 'yes' or 'no'. The rune she draws is Uruz in its upright position. Think what animal is represented by this rune, and what picture springs to mind. Think of the keywords. What do you make of this? Would you agree if I suggested that this meant that hard work in her present job would pay off, or would you suggest that an element of sacrifice might be necessary (i.e. to give up her secure job and leap into the unknown). It's not always easy to come up with a definite answer, is it! What would the difference be if the Uruz rune had been drawn in its inverted position?

Practising with sigils

Now let's practise forming a sigil or runeword. You go to a craft fair and meet someone who makes jewellery. You explain to him your interest in runic symbolism and that you would love to have a

necklace made up with your name on in runic symbolism. Your name is Karan (hint – note the spelling). You work as a secretary, but have landed an audition for a possible singing contract. It could lead to big things and you want to have as much help as you can when you go for the audition.

Look at the runes and decide which runes you would use. Remember that there is a different linkage with the runic symbols and English lettering when you are doing name work. Remember also that you may wish to choose the Anglo-Saxon symbols rather than the Germanic ones we have mainly discussed in this book.

What leader rune would you use before the name, and what sealer rune afterwards?

If I suggested Laguz, Kaunaz, Ansuz, Raido, Ansuz, Nauthiz and Gebo, would you agree? Am I right or wrong? Remember that you would have to draw the symbol clearly for the jeweller, as he probably wouldn't have a clue about the runic script. Practise drawing the symbols. Check what you have put. Might you consider changing your name? Would it be advisable to look at numerological links before deciding what name to choose? It's all your decision.

Looking for help when unwell

Sticking with the thought of forming sigils or runewords, let us now think back to runes used for healing.

Sara is not well. She seems to suffer with headaches. The doctor thinks it's all due to tension, and you know how wound up she gets over the slightest thing and you want to help her to calm down. You suggest, amongst other things, that she uses the runes. What single rune would you suggest she uses, which might help her? How would you react if I suggested Algiz? Is that appropriate, do you think? Would you suggest she tries to meditate with this rune? Would meditation help her to calm down? How would you explain this to her, if she has never meditated before?

You decide to help further by giving her a present of some jewellery with a healing sigil engraved upon it. There are two we have discussed, one for physical things and one for more emotional things. Which would you use, on the assumption that you could only use one? Again, is there a clear answer here?

Fed up with practising? Maybe you would like to do your own reading now and see what you come up with. Remember to try to be objective, which isn't always easy when you are working for yourself or for someone who is close to you and you know well.

Some runemasters suggest that you shouldn't do your own castings, in much the same way as people suggest you shouldn't do your own Tarot or I Ching readings. Again, this is a personal choice. I don't hold any firm views one way or another, but I suggest that you consider using a different set of runes for others to that which you use for yourself.

We have now covered most basic aspects of the runes. There is still a lot we could learn, but that comes after grasping the essentials.

A NOTE OF CAUTION

Before we finish this book, it is important that we discuss how using the runes can cause problems. This can only happen if we get things wrong, and that is why it is essential that you learn and fully understand what you are doing.

Nordic saga tells of a young man who scored a runic sigil on a piece of whalebone in an attempt to help with the healing of a young girl. From the moment she was given the whalebone, she became worse rather than better. This was discovered by another young man called Egil, who was a great warrior and poet. He removed the runic symbols from the whalebone and then burnt it, replacing it with something else on which the correct symbols were carved. The girl duly got better.

All this may have little foundation in modern lives, but it is worth mentioning because it serves to highlight the importance of getting things right. In the same way as this girl failed to improve, by your giving an incorrect interpretation to a rune casting, the person you are seeking to help may in fact be hindered. It is important to remember that at all times, and to be sure what you are saying, and more so how you are saying it. Irrespective of whether you are a professional or not, the responsibility that is carried is the same. You are seeking to provide help. That must be the main aim at all times. You are not seeking to scare someone, nor must you let them go away feeling unhappy with what has been given.

You must never force a runic casting on anybody. Some people will not feel happy with runes; some will. Make sure you are offering something with which the person concerned feels comfortable. You may wish to try drawing one rune in answer to the question, 'Should I do a runic reading for this person?' See what answer you get. If the answer is No, then leave it.

If you are seeking to write a runic sigil, make sure that the thing makes sense. Learning to write runic protection sigils can be very complicated, and other than those we have given, it is best left to those who have studied this in greater detail than we have been able to give here. Messing about with runes for 'magical' purposes can unleash things with which you may not be able to deal, in the same way as messing about with anything can be dangerous, so be warned. As we said at the outset, runes are not toys, and should be treated with respect. There are indeed some serious students of the runes who suggest that we should not even try to use them to help us in our daily lives. I disagree strongly on this, however, as it wastes the power of the runes. The Vikings used them in this way, and provided we know what we are doing and serve to do it correctly, no harm can come – in fact just the opposite. Anything which can help us to contact our inner selves can only be worthwhile, surely!

If you are interested in further study of the runes, their symbolism, runic poetry or the history of the runes, consult the further reading list at the end of this book.

May the runes guide you on your journey of self-discovery and enlightenment both in Midgard (our material universe) and beyond.

fURTbER READING

Blum, Ralph, *The book of Runes*, Oracle Books, Los Angeles, 1982

Cooper, D. Jason, *Using the Runes*, Aquarian, London, 1988

Dickens, Bruce, *The Runic and Heroic Poems*, Cambridge University Press, 1915

Howard, Michael, *The Magic of the Runes*, Sam Weiser, New York, 1980

Pennick, Nigel, *Runic Astrology*, Aquarian, London, 1990

Rodrigues, Louis, *Anglo-Saxon Verse Runes*, Llanerch Publishers, Felinfach, 1992

Thorsson, Edred, *Nine Doors of Midgard*, Llewellyn, Minnesota, 1991

Those people interested in alphabets and their numerological connection *must* read: Nigel Pennick *The Secret Lore of Runes and Other Ancient Alphabets*, Rider, London, 1991